Hitler's Heroes During The Defeat in the East

Hitler's Heroes During The Defeat in the East

Knight's Cross Generals on the Eastern Front, 13 February 1944–9 May 1945

Jeremy Dixon

Frontline Books

First published in Great Britain in 2025 by
Frontline Books
An imprint of Pen & Sword Books Limited
Yorkshire – Philadelphia

ISBN 978 1 03610 275 3

A CIP catalogue record for this book is
available from the British Library.

Typeset by Mac Style
Printed in the UK by CPI Group (UK) Ltd, Croydon, CR0 4YY.

MIX
Paper | Supporting responsible forestry
FSC® C013604

The Publisher's authorised representative in the EU for product
safety is Authorised Rep Compliance Ltd., Ground Floor,
71 Lower Baggot Street, Dublin D02 P593, Ireland.
www.arccompliance.com

For a complete list of Pen & Sword titles please contact

PEN & SWORD BOOKS LIMITED
47 Church Street, Barnsley, South Yorkshire, S70 2AS, England
E-mail: enquiries@pen-and-sword.co.uk
Website: www.pen-and-sword.co.uk
or
PEN AND SWORD BOOKS
1950 Lawrence Road, Havertown, PA 19083, USA
E-mail: uspen-and-sword@casematepublishers.com
Website: www.penandswordbooks.com

Dedicated to Angela Axton-Green

Contents

Acknowledgements

I would like to thank Paul Budden for proof-reading the book, as well as offering advice and encouragement and I must also thank my mum and dad, sister and nephews for their continued support. I would also like to thank my friends for their interest, and my thanks go to Ann Driscoll, Anne Taylor, Jo Robinson, Jo Jeffrey, Emily Budgen, Nick Isles, Hazel Kirby, Jackie Snowling, Carol Ryan, Laura Fisher, Lisa Hunt, Tracy Dover, Jane Budgen, Kelly Delroy, Bev Drew, Gemma Ross, Nicola Willoughby, Josie Hobson, Lauretta Kelly, Daniella Craig, Vanessa Gardner, Linda Hurd, Colin Harris, Alex Curran, Nathan and Emma Pearce.

Introduction

Generaloberst Walter Model.

This is a four-volume study that describes how 552 German officers who held the rank of General won the Knight's Cross, the highest award for command and bravery. The fourth and final volume describes how 115 generals (eighteen full Generals; fifty-eight Generalleutnants and thirty-nine Generalmajors) won the award during the last three months of the German invasion of the Soviet Union.

By the beginning of February 1944 the Germans had lost the war in the Soviet Union and were still very much on the retreat, in fact the entire east bank of Lake Peipus had been cleared of German troops. Russian units reached a point within 45 miles of Pskov in north-western Russia and the city controlled the approaches to Latvia. German Army Group North, under the command of *Generaloberst* Walter Model, began to withdraw from the Russian Narva–Newel front.

On 21 February Soviet troops pressed forward in the Lake Ilmen area and the next day Krivoy Rog fell to the Red Army, returning control of the entire Ukrainian industrial area to the Soviets. On 5 March the Soviets launched an offensive against the Germans in order to drive them out of the Dnieper Bend in Ukraine under the command of General Zhukov. Four days later, Soviet troops advanced to Tarnopol, where house-to-house fighting took place, and by the 10th, Soviet forces occupied Berslav in their drive to the Dnieper. On the 15th Soviet forces broke through German defences on the Bug River and advanced along a broad front. On 1 April, 40,000 German troops were trapped by the Soviets in the town of Skala in Ukraine, and over the next nine days a total of 26,000 Germans were killed. Even now Hitler still continued to believe in victory over the Russians, stating: 'The Russians have exhausted and divided their forces.'

On 7 April German forces made a counter-attack in the Crimea and suffered heavy casualties. The following day the Soviets launched the final drive to oust the Germans from the Crimea. Three days later the Black Sea port of Odessa was recaptured by Soviet forces after fierce fighting with German forces of Army Group A under the command of *General der Gebirgstruppe* Ferdinand Schörner. On the 11th the German 17th Army, under the command of *Generaloberst* Erwin Jaenecke, fell back to Sevastopol as the Red Army took Kerch in a new offensive, also retaking Crimea. Within two days the Red Army had reoccupied Simferopol in the Crimea and had captured more than 20,000 German troops.

General der Gebirgstruppe Ferdinand Schörner.

On 9 May Soviet troops liberated Sevastopol from the Germans, the main naval base of the Black Sea Fleet, and three days later the last German troops were evacuated from the Crimea. Soviet troops began their summer offensive on 22 June, they amassed 146 infantry divisions and forty-three tank brigades along a 300-mile front aimed at Vitebsk. The action ended a comparative lull while the Soviets and Germans regrouped in preparation for a new round of fighting. By the 24th Soviet troops had reached the Dvina River on the Baltic front, and two days later Vitebsk fell to the Soviets. The following day five German divisions were trapped as Soviet troops cut the road between Smolensk and Minsk by encircling Vitebsk. German Army Group Centre, under the command of *Generalfeldmarschall* Ernst Busch, broke under the assault. Two days later 80,000 German soldiers were captured. Stalin ordered Moscow's 224 guns to fire in order to mark the first major victory of the summer offensive and Soviet troops crossed the Dnieper River. On 3 July Minsk was recaptured by Soviet forces and Moscow proclaimed 'one of the decisive victories of the war!'

Generaloberst Erwin Jaenecke.

On 10 July Hitler refused to permit the withdrawal of Army Group North behind the Dvina River, as recommended by *Generaloberst* Model. The German 9th and 4th Armies had already been virtually annihilated. On 19 July five German divisions were trapped west of Brody in Ukraine and three days later German forces in the Brody Pocket were virtually destroyed, which included the 18th Artillery Division under the command of *Generalleutnant* Karl Thoholte. On 23 July the last Soviet pre-war city held by the Germans, Pskov, was recaptured by the Soviets and *Generaloberst* Ferdinand Schörner replaced *Generaloberst* Johannes Friessner as Commander-in-Chief of Army Group North. By 7 August the Soviets had advanced from the Dnieper to the Vistula which was a distance of more than 400 miles. However, they had wanted to advance even further but had overextended their supply lines.

Generalfeldmarschall Ernst Busch.

Generaloberst Johannes Friessner.

On 20 August a major Soviet offensive began in the south with two main attacks near Jassy-Kishinev and Tiraspol. The German forces of Army Group South were attacked by Soviet fighters in the north in Latvia and two days later Jassy-Kishinev was taken by Soviet troops, who had advanced more than 50 miles in just two days. The Soviet forces in the south advanced at great speed and *Generaloberst* Friessner's Army Group South Ukraine was shattered by Soviet attacks and the defection of the Romanians. On 29 August the Soviets took the important Black Sea port of Constanta, and Ploesti fell the following day. On 16 September there was a large-scale Soviet offensive in the Baltic States involving attacks against Riga and Tallinn, and by the 23rd the Soviets had reached the Baltic at Pärnu. Two days later they took the Estonian port of Haapsalu, meaning German resistance on the Estonian mainland was over. By 2 October the brave resistance of the forces in Warsaw had come to an end and at least 200,000 Poles had died during the brutal fighting. A few weeks later the Soviets expelled the last German troops from Saaremo Island in the Gulf of Riga and the remaining heavy units of the German Navy, *Lützow*, *Admiral Scheer* and *Prinz Eugen*, had covered the evacuation of the 5,000 German troops.

Generaloberst Georg-Hans Reinhardt.

Generaloberst Lothar Rendulic.

On 12 January 1945 a major Soviet offensive began all along the front from the Baltic to the Carpathians. The Soviets attacked with nine armies north of Warsaw and there were additional efforts by the 2nd and 3rd Belorussian Armies on both Baltic Fronts against the German forces in East Prussia. The defending German forces were mainly from Army Group Centre and Army Group A, and the 2nd Army would bear the brunt of the attack. The German forces were outnumbered by at least four or five to one in all classes of equipment and had no real answer to the Red Army's power, resulting in all German defence lines along the front in Poland being shattered by these attacks. The Soviet offences now began to achieve important successes and they cut the rail line at Kracow, and further south in Hungary, the Soviets attempted to push the Germans out of Budapest. On 20 January the Soviet offensive against the Germans in East Prussia achieved an important breakthrough and Tilsit was taken. All the Soviet fronts in Poland were moving forward despite German resistance and five days later German forces in East Prussia were virtually cut off and evacuation operations started, which would continue into April. There were considerable losses to the many mines laid in the Baltic by RAF Bomber Command and to the submarines of the Soviet Baltic Fleet. *Generaloberst* Georg-Hans Reinhardt, the commander of the German Army Group Centre in East Prussia, was dismissed and *Generaloberst* Lothar Rendulic was appointed to the renamed Army Group North.

On 7 February Russian General Georgy Zhukov's troops on the Oder seized small bridgeheads over the river in the area around Furstenberg. In East Prussia

German forces had now been virtually split into three groups: the defenders of Königsberg, some forces trapped on the peninsula to the west of the town and those to the south, the largest group, were holding out near Heiligenbeil. By 10 February the last German resistance in Elbing had come to an end and the town was occupied by troops of the Soviet army. The Soviets moved northward into German Pomerania on a 200-mile front and the Germans opposing them were from Himmler's Army Group Vistula, whose incompetence contributed to their plight. On 23 February Poznan fell to the Red Army after a twenty-eight-day battle. During constant Soviet attacks into East Pomerania and counter-attacks near Stettin, the Germans began to evacuate their wounded and refugees from Kolberg. By 10 March the German advance had been slowed by the fierce Soviet ground forces and air patrols, as well as the terrible muddy conditions and lack of fuel. On the 18th the Soviets took Kolberg and moved further towards the German positions in East Prussia. Two days later Soviet forces in the Stettin area eliminated the German bridgehead over the Oder. *Generaloberst* Gotthard Heinrici, one of the best defensive tacticians in the German Army, was appointed Commander-in-Chief of Army Group Vistula, taking over from Himmler. Heinrici now had the task of building up defences along the Oder for when the Soviets extended their advance toward Berlin, but the Army Group had already lost a large part of its original force in the fighting in Pomerania. By the 27th the Soviets had penetrated the final defences at both Gdynia and Danzig. The attacks went on for three days until the final German positions in Danzig were overcome by Soviet attacks.

On 6 April Soviet forces began to besiege Vienna and, despite German counter-attacks, they pushed into Austria and East Prussia, with the Soviet attacks on Königsberg beginning to break through the defences. Finally, on 9 April, the German defenders surrendered to the Red Army, and four days later Vienna fell. On the 16th *Generaloberst* Heinrici's Army Group Vistula and *Generalfeldmarschall* Ferdinand Schörner's Army Group Centre made ready for the onslaught of a massive Soviet attack west of the Oder near Küstrin. The following day the Soviet attacks east of Berlin continued and in very fierce fighting, the Germans were slowly forced to give ground. On the 21st Soviet tanks from Zhukov's command reached the eastern suburbs of Berlin, and three days later they

Generaloberst Gotthard Heinrici.

General der Infanterie Hans Krebs.

entered the city from the south and the east. Templehof airfield was taken by the Soviets and by the 28th their forces were only one mile from Hitler's bunker. The following day Hitler was married to Eva Braun and named *Grossadmiral* Karl Dönitz of the German Navy his successor as the Soviets got nearer and nearer. Just ten days after their marriage, Hitler and Braun committed suicide and their bodies were cremated as the Soviet advance in Berlin reached the Reichstag.

On 1 May the Chief of the Army General Staff, *General der Infanterie* Hans Krebs, visited General Zhukov to try to negotiate surrender terms for Berlin, but he was told that only unconditional surrender would be acceptable. When Krebs returned to his headquarters he committed suicide.

The following day Soviet forces completed the capture of Berlin with attacks from the north and south, and the following day Soviet forces reached the Elbe west of Berlin and made contact with the US 1st and 9th Armies and in the south with the British 2nd Army. On 4 May the new head of the German Government, *Grossadmiral* Dönitz, sent envoys to Montgomery's headquarters at Luneburg Heath and they agreed surrender terms, and the following day at 0800 hours the German surrender came into force. The 8 May was announced as Victory in Europe Day, however the Soviet Union celebrated the following day – the war in Europe was finally over.

Knight's Cross Recipients

Recipients in order of being awarded.

NB: Underlined Christian names are those the subject chose to be known by.

<u>Georg</u> Karl Hermann Edmund Graf von RITTBERG
Generalleutnant

* 30 May 1898, Strassbourg
+ 6 June 1973, Krün

Knight's Cross: Awarded on 21 February 1944 as *Generalmajor* and Commander of the 88th Infantry Division for his role in commanding part of the rearguard during the breakout of German forces from the Cherkassy Pocket between 24 January and 16 February 1944. During this time he helped shield the flanks and rear of the retreating German divisions before breaking out with his own troops following a hard-fought attack near Potschapinzy in Ukraine. Rittberg

Georg Graf von Rittberg entered the 2nd Grand Ducal Hessian Field Artillery Regiment in August 1914 as an officer candidate and was commissioned as a *Leutnant* in May 1915. He served during the First World War as a battery officer and later as an ordnance officer, ending the war as an adjutant with Field Artillery Regiment 61. He stayed with the Army after the war, serving with the cavalry for a time, and from October 1935, now with the rank of *Hauptmann*, he served as a battalion commander with Artillery Regiment 31 in Potsdam. From April 1939 he was an adjutant on the Staff of the commanding general of the Wehrmacht in the Reich Protectorate of Bohemia and Moravia (occupied Czechoslovakia). In May 1940 he was commander of Artillery Regiment 31, now with the rank of *Oberstleutnant*, and later took command of the 23rd Artillery regiment. From April 1943 he took command of the 2nd Grenadier Regiment.

successfully led his division and they were rested for a time in Poland before being back in action once again in the summer, when Rittberg on 1 August was promoted to *Generalleutnant*.

Knight's Cross with Oakleaves: Rittberg became the 610th recipient on 10 October 1944 as *Generalmajor* and Commander of the 88th Infantry Division in recognition of his leadership during the fighting in the summer of 1944 near the great Vistula bend. Here his men managed to push back Soviet forces and build up their own defensive positions south of Opatów in Poland, and during the fighting at the Baranov Bridgehead on the Vistula his division destroyed more than 100 Soviet tanks. Rittberg was presented with the Oakleaves by *SS-Reichsführer* Heinrich Himmler on 7 November at Posen during a special ceremony with seventeen other officers who had been awarded the Oakleaves, including *SS-Gruppenführer* Heinz Reinefarth, *Generalmajor* Werner Marcks, *Oberst* Arthur Jüttner and *Oberst* Wilhelm Bleckwenn. He later saw action during the Soviet winter offensive and in January 1945 he was wounded and taken prisoner by the Red Army. Rittberg was imprisoned in Radom, then later moved to another prison in Ukraine and then to various prisons in Krasnogorsk, Smolensk and Černcy. On 12 May 1949 he was tried by a Military Tribunal in Leningrad and sentenced to twenty-five years' forced labour. Rittberg was released early in October 1955 after a general amnesty and returned to Germany.

Adolf Eduard TROWITZ

Generalmajor

* 24 September 1893, Dessau
+ 3 January 1978, Hamburg

Knight's Cross: Awarded on 21 February 1944 as *Generalmajor* and Commander of the 57th Infantry

Adolf Trowitz entered the Army in March 1914 and was attached to the I. Battalion of Artillery Regiment 4, later serving as battalion adjutant. He left the Army in 1925, rejoined as a *Hauptmann* in April 1934 and served with various artillery regiments. He was promoted to *Oberstleutnant* in October 1939 and served as commander of Artillery Regiment Staff 603. From March 1942 he was Artillery Commander 105 with the rank of *Oberst*. He attended a divisional leaders' course from May 1943 and later took command of the 322nd Infantry Division.

Division for his leadership during the Dnieper withdrawal and the heavy fighting before his division was encircled at Cherkassy. He led it during a breakout with heavy losses of life and equipment and was soon after sent to Poland to regroup and to rebuild, with its artillery partially re-equipped with captured French guns. The division soon returned to action while attached to Army Group Centre and made ready for the Soviet summer offensive. The division was surrounded near Minsk in July and Trowitz was captured on 7 July and remained in Soviet captivity until a general amnesty, upon which he was released on 8 October 1955 and returned to Germany.

Karl Hermann Ludwig BURDACH

Generalleutnant

* 28 July 1891, Chemnitz, Saxony
+ 30 December 1976, Freiburg im Breisgau, Baden-Württemberg

Knight's Cross: Awarded on 23 February 1944 as *Generalleutnant* and Commander of the 11th Infantry Division as part of the L. Army Corps for his outstanding leadership of his division during the fighting on the northern sector of the Eastern Front in early 1944. His command was able to defeat all Soviet attempts to encircle his command and played a major role in the relatively smooth withdrawal to Lake Peipus on the border of Estonia and the Soviet Union. From June 1944 Burdach was attached to Army Group

Karl Burdach entered the Army in April 1912 with Field Artillery Regiment 12 and was commissioned as a *Leutnant* a year later. From April 1915 he served as adjutant of the I. Battalion of his regiment and was promoted to *Oberleutnant* in January 1917. Shortly after, he was made temporary battery leader before being appointed adjutant. He stayed in the Army after the war and by October 1935 was serving as commander of the II. Battalion of Artillery Regiment 50. Promoted to *Oberst* in April 1937, he was appointed Chief of the Department for Replacement Affairs from October while attached to the Reich War Ministry. At the beginning of the war in September 1939 he was commander of Artillery Regiment 194 and from April 1940 was appointed Artillery Commander 123, seeing action in France. From August 1941, now with the rank of *Generalmajor*, he took command of the 251st Infantry Division, seeing action during the invasion of the Soviet Union.

North Ukraine and the following month he was appointed temporary Higher Artillery Commander 311, which became permanent from 5 July 1944. He saw action on the Eastern Front as part of Panzer Group 1 under the command of *General der Panzertruppe* Erhard Raus. After a brief period in the Reserves, he was appointed Higher Artillery Commander 320 from September 1944 and saw action in the Netherlands as part of the 15th Army until his command surrendered to US troops in the Ruhr District on 17 April 1945.

Hans-Ludwig SPETH

General der Artillerie

* 7 October 1897, Rockenberg, Friedberg
+ 30 April 1985, Gauting, Munich

Knight's Cross: Awarded on 23 February 1944 as *Generalleutnant* and Commander of the 28th *Jäger* Division, part of the XXXVIII. Army Corps, for actions during the heavy fighting in the Second Battle of Lake Ladoga near Leningrad. On 28 April Speth relinquished his command and after four weeks of leave he was named as the Commander of the War Academy in Berlin. He was promoted to the rank of *General der Artillerie* in October 1944, and remained commander of the Academy until the end of the war.

Hans-Ludwig Speth was a war volunteer from July 1915 and served with Mountain Battery 16, being commissioned as a *Leutnant* in December 1917. He remained in the Army after the war, serving with Artillery Regiment 6 in Hannover, and from October 1931 he served on the Staff of the 4th Division in Dresden. In October 1935 he was company commander with Artillery Regiment 14 in Naumburg and was promoted to *Major* in April 1936. From August 1936 he served as an instructor at the War Academy in Berlin and from August 1939 he was Chief of Operations of the XXVII. Army Corps, now with the rank of *Oberstleutnant*. He was later assigned to the German Army Mission in Romania and later served as the German Liaison Officer in Albania. From November 1942 he was Chief of the General Staff of the 18th Army.

Bruno Anton Theodor FRANKEWITZ

Generalleutnant

* 8 December 1897, Tiefensee, West Prussia
+ 11 August 1982, Straehlen

Knight's Cross: Awarded on 29 February 1944 as *Generalleutnant* and Commander of the 215th Infantry Division, attached to the L. Army Corps in recognition of his bravery and leadership during the fighting around Pushkin in the Soviet Union between 15 and 24 January. In February his division played a vital role in building the German front, creating a new defensive line between Luga Wyriza near Leningrad during a three-day defensive battle with the Red Army.

Knight's Cross with Oakleaves: Awarded on 16 March 1945 as *Generalleutnant* and became the 790th recipient while still Commander of the 215th Infantry Division, in recognition of his leadership during the heavy battles in the Courland area, particularly south of Frombork in Poland. Here his command repelled a total of 111 enemy attacks, mostly at regimental level, between 21 and 27 December 1944. Frankewitz had especially distinguished himself in the fighting around Daugavpils in Latvia. On 6 April he was chosen to command the Reich Labour Service Division 'Theodor Körner', with staff from the disbanded 215th Infantry Division. It comprised of about 10,000 men, with 7,500 provided by the Reich Labour Service, and was part of the XX. Army Corps, seeing action

Bruno Frankewitz entered the Army as a war volunteer in Guard Foot Artillery Regiment 2 and was commissioned as a *Leutnant der Reserve* in June 1916. He ended the war as leader of the 1st Company with Assault Detachment von Michelmann and in May 1920 he transferred to the police and served in Dortmund and in Arnsberg, rising to the rank of *Polizei-Hauptmann*. In March 1935 he re-entered the Army and was given command of the Personnel Staff of Artillery Regiment Fulda, later becoming battery commander with Artillery Regiment 29. Promoted to *Major* in March 1936, he was appointed battalion commander with Artillery Regiment 37, and August 1939 he took command of Artillery Regiment 161. He saw action during the invasion of Poland, where he was awarded both classes of the Bar to the Iron Cross. He later saw action during the invasion of France and Belgium from May 1940, and later during the invasion of the Soviet Union from June 1941.

just south of Berlin against Soviet and Western Allied troops. On 7 May 1945 Frankewitz surrendered to Western Allied troops and remained in captivity until his release in July 1947.

Max REINWALD

Generalmajor der Reserve

* 1 September 1903, Hagelstadt, Regensburg
+ 8 June 1969, Regensburg

Knight's Cross: Awarded on 29 February 1944 as *Oberstleutnant der Reserve* and Commander of Grenadier Regiment 19 for his leadership during the heavy defensive battles in the Pripyat Marshes near Rechytsa in the Soviet Union. On 14 January Soviet forces attacked Reinwald's Grenadier regiment from all sides, but every assault was unsuccessful. Then, with Reinwald at the front, he led his men in a successful attack against Soviet forces. This enabled the Germans to form a new defensive line and he was presented with the Knight's Cross in early March by the Commander of the 7th Infantry Division, *Generalleutnant* Fritz-Georg Rappard.

Knight's Cross with Oakleaves: Awarded on 18 January 1945 to become the 702nd recipient as *Oberst der Reserve* and Commander of Grenadier Regiment 19 while attached to the 7th Infantry Division for actions on the Eastern Front. It was awarded mainly for Reinwald's leadership during the Soviet summer

Max Reinwald entered the Officers' Training School in Fürstenfeldbruck in October 1917 and was assigned to Infantry Regiment 20 from September 1920. He retired from the Army with the rank of Oberfeldwebel in 1931 and re-entered four years later as a Reserve Officer with the rank of *Leutnant* and took part in the invasion of Austria and Czechoslovakia. He served as company commander with Infantry Regiment 19 from September 1939, seeing action in Poland and later in 1940 fought in Belgium. He was promoted to *Hauptmann der Reserve* in January 1942, seeing action in the Soviet Union, and from March he took command of the III. Battalion of Infantry Regiment 19. He later took command of the I. Battalion, and from April 1943 was given the leadership of Grenadier Regiment 61 and promoted to *Oberstleutnant der Reserve* in October 1943.

offensive and his command particularly distinguished itself during the fighting near Narew, which began on 10 October 1944. During the next few days the Soviet 48th Army launched as many as thirty attacks against the Germans with artillery and air support, but the German forces successfully held them back, even though Reinwald's position had been bombed by the Soviet air force. In November Reinwald attended a divisional leaders' course in Hirschberg and from January 1945 he was named Leader of the 362nd Infantry Division in Italy. He was promoted to *Generalmajor der Reserve* in April and he was confirmed as Commander of the 362nd Infantry Division, where he continued to see action in Italy. There, on 2 May 1945, he surrendered to Allied forces, being released on 7 July 1947.

Curt Karl SIEWERT
Generalleutnant

* 5 April 1899, Forsthaus Ratzburg, Ortelsburg
\+ 13 June 1983, Hannover

Knight's Cross: Awarded on 29 February 1944 as *Generalmajor* and Commander of the 58th Infantry Division while attached to Army Group North, seeing action in Estonia on the extreme southern flank near Nevel, Estonia, against tough Soviet troops. In January 1944 his division was ordered back to the north but arrived too late to prevent the Soviets from breaking the siege at Leningrad. His

Curt Siewert entered the Royal Prussian Army in December 1916 and served throughout the First World War with the same regiment, being commissioned as a *Leutnant* in February 1918. He served in the *Reichswehr* from 1920 while attached to Prussian Infantry Regiment 5, and from 1930 he served in the Reich defence Ministry in Berlin and was promoted to *Hauptmann* in June 1933. From April 1938, now with the rank of *Major*, Siewert served as adjutant to *Generaloberst* Walter von Brauchitsch, the Commander-in-Chief of the Army. From February 1941 he served as Chief of the General Staff of the XXXVIII. Army Corps and was promoted to *Oberst* in December that same year. In September 1943, with the rank of *Generalmajor*, he was appointed commander of the 58th Infantry Division and was assigned to the Russian Front.

command lost one third of its men and all its heavy equipment during the rushed withdrawal from the city, and in July he was promoted to *Generalleutnant*. Siewert, however, managed to fight at Narva and at Daugavpils in February 1945 his command returned to the central sector and became cut off in the Samland region of East Prussia. On 13 April Siewert was seriously wounded in action and was medically evacuated to Germany, where he was captured by the Western Allies in early May 1945. In October 1956 he rejoined the army with the *Bundeswehr* as a *Generalmajor* and was initially commander of the I. Corps and from January 1958 he was appointed Commander in Military Area II. He later wrote a book entitled, *Guilty? The Generals Under Hitler.*

Wilhelm Otto Ferdinand BERLIN

General der Artillerie

* 28 April 1889, Cologne
+ 15 September 1987, Hamburg

Knight's Cross: Awarded on 6 March 1944 as *Generalleutnant* and Commander of the 227th Infantry Division for outstanding leadership during the heavy fighting during the Battle of Narva in Estonia on the Eastern Front as part of Army Group North. In February Berlin was given temporary command of Group '*Sponheimer*' and in May he took over as temporary commander of the XXVI. Army Corps. From July until November he was attached to the

Wilhelm Berlin entered Army service with Foot Artillery Regiment 14 in March 1909, and was commissioned as a *Leutnant* the following year. At the start of the First World War he was serving as signals officer of Fortress 'Kaiser Wilhelm II', one of the fortifications built by Germany at the end of the nineteenth century to defend Strasbourg. He later served on the Staff of XV. Reserve Corps and in February 1915 he was promoted to *Oberleutnant*. From July he was company leader in Foot Artillery Regiment 14. He stayed in the Army after the war, serving mainly with Artillery Regiment 5, and then from May 1936 he served with the new Panzer Troops. At the start of the Second World War he served as Artillery Commander 101 with the rank of *Oberst*, and later served as commander of Artillery School II in Jüterbog and was promoted to *Generalmajor* in March 1940. From April 1943 he was commander of the 58th Infantry Division and two months later, now with the rank of *Generalleutnant*, he took command of the 227th Infantry Division.

Chief of the Army General Staff, under *Generaloberst* Heinz Guderian, and had been promoted to *General der Artillerie* in October. On 27 February 1945 he took over as temporary Commander of the CI. Army Corps, seeing action near the Oder area north-west of Küstrin, and from 18 April he was once again attached to the High Command of the Army. He was captured by US troops on 8 May, being released in July 1947.

Heinrich Gustav Hellmuth PRIESS

General der Infanterie

* 6 March 1896, Hildesheim, Lower Saxony
+ 21 October 1944 near Hasenrode, East Prussia

Knight's Cross: Awarded on 7 March 1944 as *Generalleutnant* and Commander of the 121st Infantry Division in recognition of his leadership and bravery during the retreat from Leningrad through the Baltic States. He also took part in the Battle of Pskov in June 1944 and during this time he was also appointed deputy leader of the XXXVIII. Army Corps. From July he took over as Commanding General of the XXVII.

Hellmuth Priess entered the Army in August 1914 as a war volunteer and was commissioned as a *Leutnant* in June 1915, and the following year was appointed leader of Field Machine-Gun Platoon 250. He stayed in the Army after the war and served with several regiments before entering the Staff of 2nd Division in Stettin with the rank of *Hauptmann*. In 1935 he was attached to the 19th Infantry Regiment in Munich and in March 1937 he was appointed Chief of Operations of the 15th Infantry Division.

Priess with the Hitler Youth Leader Artur Axmann [left]. At the start of the Second World War Priess was attached to the Department of National Defence with the High Command of the Army in Berlin and was promoted to *Oberst* in October 1940. From March 1942 he as commander of Infantry Regiment 671 and from November he took command of the 121st Infantry Division.

Army Corps, which had been reformed as the majority of its forces, including its Commander, *General der Infanterie* Paul Völckers, had been taken prisoner by Soviet troops. Priess re-established a new XXVII. Army Corps and was deployed to defend the East Prussian border, and in October 1944 he was promoted to *General der Infanterie*. On 21 October he was killed when his aircraft was shot down in the Hasenrode area south of Gumbinnen, East Prussia, where his body was discovered a few days later.

Dr Karl KOSKE
Generalmajor

* 27 June 1889, Sarajevo, Austro-Hungary
+ 8 April 1945, Vienna, Austria

Knight's Cross: Awarded on 15 March 1944 as *Generalmajor* and Commander of the 212th Infantry Division for his leadership during the attack against the German lines in Luga near Leningrad in February 1944. The Soviets succeeded in splintering the German units and cutting off their supply routes located near Sparrow Hills, one of the highest points near Moscow, and this move rendered any retreat of artillery, heavy weapons and other supplies impossible. Koske found his position in a precarious situation, made no easier by the ongoing attacks and with this in mind he scraped together a battle force. With this force he managed to restore both land communications and his supply routes via a counter-attack from both the east and west. Due to his considered

Karl Koske entered the Austrian Army as a one-year volunteer and in August 1914 he was called up from the Reserves as a *Leutnant* and served during the war as a battery officer. He ended the war as an *Oberleutnant* with Field Artillery Regiment 35 and remained in the Army, rising to the rank of *Major* in September 1927 and attending various courses. In March 1938 he transferred into the German Army as a result of the Union with Germany, and was assigned to Army Group Command 5. At the beginning of the Second World War he was attached to Heavy Artillery Battalion 643 and was promoted to *Oberst* in December 1940. From April 1942 he served as Artillery Commander 18 and then from November 1943 he took command of the 212th Infantry Division.

command, the German attack of heavy machine guns and mortar fire provided stability and calm among his troops. He managed to make contact with cut-off elements of his command and they pushed their way through the heavy Soviet mortar fire to a safer defensive position. His grenadiers conducted themselves outstandingly, and brought bloody losses upon the Red Army, including the virtual annihilation of a Soviet rifle division. However, in early May 1944 Koseke was taken ill with angina pectoris, a form of heart disease, and was relieved of his command. By the end of September he had recovered enough and was attached to the Reich War Courts, but was not well enough to return to front-line duty. In November he was appointed a judge at the Reich War Courts in Austria and in March 1945 he was taken ill once again and killed in a hospital in Vienna during an Allied air raid on 8 April 1945.

Hans KISSEL

Generalmajor

* 19 February 1897, Mannheim
+ 30 December 1975, Königstein

Knight's Cross: Awarded on 17 March 1944 as *Oberst* and Commander of Grenadier Regiment 683 while attached to the 335th Infantry Division for actions and bravery during the heavy fighting in the Dnieper Bend battles and in the Zaporozhye Bridgehead. On 25 September 1944 he was appointed commander of Grenadier Regiment 178 while attached to the 76th Infantry Division. Kissel saw action in the Groβwardein district in western Romania, where he was severely wounded on 10 November 1944. He never

Hans Kissel entered the Army in September 1915 with Infantry Regiment 142 and was commissioned as a *Leutnant* in January 1917. He served as a platoon and company leader and later as an adjutant. He left the Army in April 1919 and rejoined in January 1935 with the rank of *Hauptmann* and served as a company commander with Infantry Regiment 34. From July 1936 he was a battalion commander with Infantry Regiment 109 with the rank of *Major* and later served with Infantry Regiment 228 and 229. He was severely wounded and hospitalised from June 1942 and returned to active duty as a battle group leader with the rank of *Oberst* in March 1943.

returned to front-line duty but was, however, promoted to *Generalmajor* on 30 January 1945 and was appointed Chief of the Operations Staff of the Berlin *Volkssturm* until the end of the war.

Johann-Georg RICHERT

Generalleutnant

* 14 April 1890, Liebau, Landeshut
+ 30 January 1946, Minsk, Soviet Union

Knight's Cross: Awarded on 17 March 1944 as *Generalleutnant* and Commander of the 35th Infantry Division as part of the 4th Army for actions on the Russian Front. At the beginning of January 1944 his division occupied new defensive positions south of Mogilev, where his forces were able to repel all Soviet attacks, and on 14 February the Soviets were forced to call off an attempted breakthrough because of Richert and his command.

Knight's Cross with Oakleaves: He became the 623rd recipient on 18 October 1944 as *Generalleutnant* and Commander of the 35th Infantry Division for his leadership and achievements made during Operation Bagration, the German offensive in Soviet Byelorussia. Under his leadership his division was able to break out of the Soviet trap near Osemlja, south of Bobruisk, in late June 1944, having destroyed sixty-eight Soviet tanks. Richert proved to be an excellent commander and his troops broke through Soviet lines to reach Brest-Litovsk.

Johann-Georg Richert entered the Army in 1909 as an officer candidate with the East Prussian Infantry Regiment No. 44 and was attached to the War School. He was commissioned as a *Leutnant* in March 1911 and served as a platoon and company leader in the First World War before being captured in 1917 and spending fourteen months as a French prisoner. He remained in the Army after the war and from October 1932 served at the War School in Dresden and in 1935 he served as a battalion commander with Infantry Regiment 50. In May 1939 he served as Commander of Infantry Regiment 23 in Rastenburg with the rank of *Oberst*, and from June 1942 he was commander of the 286th Security Division, now with the rank of *Generalmajor*, and from November 1943 he took over as commander of the 35th Infantry Division.

The Oakleaves were presented personally by Hitler at the end of October 1944 at *Führer* Headquarters, the Wolf's Lair at Rastenburg. He was captured by Soviet troops on 9 May 1945 and in January the following year he was sentenced to death by a court in Minsk together with thirteen other senior German commanders. Richert had been charged over the deaths of at least twenty-eight civilians near Orsha, which included eighteen children.

Helmut Bernhard Franz BECHLER

Generalmajor

* 2 June 1898, Grün, Anerback in Saxony
+ 9 January 1971, Kassel in Northern Hesse

Knight's Cross: Awarded on 26 March 1944 as *Oberst* and Commander of Grenadier Regiment 504 as part of the 291st Infantry Division in recognition of his leadership and success during the night of 9–10 March 1944. His regiment had been tasked with occupying the village of Sapadinzy in the Soviet Union, and their mission was to hold the village and prevent the enemy from reaching the road while the bulk of the German corps was retreating. As elements of German forces arrived, they were surprised by Soviet armour and Bechler and his regiment acted swiftly to stabilise the situation, and held the village for three days against all Soviet attacks. From October until August 1944 he served as commander of Grenadier Regiment 504, having been promoted to *Oberst*. In October was given temporary command of the 275th Infantry Division,

Helmut Bechler entered military service in June 1915 with Royal Saxony Infantry Regiment 182, and was wounded in July 1916. In October that year he was commissioned as a *Leutnant*. From December he served as ordnance officer on the staff of the II. Battalion of his regiment, and remained in the Army until 1920. He rejoined the Army in July 1934 as a *Hauptmann*, being assigned to Regiment 53. From October 1935 until the beginning of the Second World War he served as company commander, and from 26 August he was commander of I. Battalion of Infantry Regiment 73, part of the 87th Infantry Division. From 10 May 1940 his battalion crossed into Belgium at the start of the Western campaign, and Bechler saw action during the Battle of France. He led his battalion into Paris and became part of the occupation force from 14 June, remaining there until the end of July.

and he led what remained of the division from Belgium and into Germany at Aachen. On 22 November he was given temporary command of the 85th Infantry Division and with his promotion to *Generalmajor* on 30 January 1945 his command was no longer temporary. He led his division during the final battles on the Belgian border with Germany. He was wounded on 15 March and taken to hospital in Königstein, being discharged in June into Soviet captivity.

Hans KREBS

General der Infanterie

* 4 March 1898, Helmstedt
+ 1 May 1945, Berlin

Knight's Cross: Awarded on 26 March 1944 as *Generalleutnant* and Chief of the General Staff of Army Group Centre for his success in the planning of the German campaign in the central sector of the Eastern Front. In August 1944 he was promoted to *General der Infanterie* and the following month he was appointed Chief of the General Staff of Army Group B under *Generalfeldmarschall* Walter Model, seeing action on the Western Front.

Knight's Cross with Oakleaves: He became the 749th recipient on 20 February 1945 as *General der Infanterie* and Chief of the General Staff of Army Group B in recognition of his excellent work and leadership as a staff officer. Shortly

Hans Krebs is seen here with *Generalfeldmarschall* Ernst Busch. Krebs entered the Army in September 1914 as a war volunteer with Jäger Battalion 10 and attended various courses before serving at the front from March 1915. Commissioned as a *Leutnant* in June, he was later wounded in action and returned to the field in August. He remained with the Army after the war, having been awarded both classes of the Iron Cross. In October 1935 he served as Chief of Operations on the General Staff of the 24th Division and two years later he served in a similar position with the High Command of the Army. Three years later he was appointed Head of the Army Household Department and shortly after he took over as Chief of the General Staff of the VII. Army Corps. In October 1940 he served at the German Embassy in Moscow with the rank of *Oberst*. In January 1942 he was Chief of the General Staff of the 9th Army and was promoted to *Generalmajor* the following month.

before he had been awarded the Knight's Cross he had returned to Zossen as the Acting Chief of the Operations Staff of the Army General Staff, succeeding *Generaloberst* Heinz Guderian. Krebs was severely wounded during a US bombing attack on Zossen on 15 March but he returned to duty on 1 April and took over as Chief of the Army General Staff. Krebs moved his headquarters to Hitler's bunker in Berlin and was present when Hitler said his final farewell before he committed suicide on 30 April. The next day Krebs left the bunker with a white flag and met up with Soviet generals in an attempt at ceasefire talks but this failed. When he returned to the bunker he informed all those present, which included Goebbels and his wife, Martin Bormann, Dr Ludwig Stumpfegger and *General der Infanterie* Wilhelm Burgdorff, what had happened. Later that day both Krebs and Burgdorff shot themselves and their bodies were later found by members of the Red Army.

Friedrich-Jobst Guido Otto VOLCKAMER VON KIRCHENSITTENBACH

General der Gebirgstruppe

* 16 April 1894, Oberstdorf, Sonthofen
+ 3 April 1989, Munich

Friedrich-Jobst Volckamer von Kirchensittenbach entered the Army in October 1913 with the 7th Company of Infantry Regiment 19 and was commissioned as a *Leutnant* in September 1914, serving as a platoon leader with Royal Bavarian Reserve Infantry Regiment 7. Promoted to *Oberleutnant* in April 1918, he served as a regimental adjutant towards the end of the war. He joined the *Freikorps* after the war and later served with various infantry regiments. From October 1932 he was a tactics instructor with the Infantry School in Dresden, now with the rank of *Hauptmann*. He first saw action during the Second World War from May 1940 as commander of Mountain Regiment 141 and now with the rank of *Oberst*. He later served as Chief of Staff of the Inspector of Education and Training in the Army and was promoted to *Generalmajor* in September 1942, when he took over as Deputy Inspector of Education and Training. From December he was appointed commander of the 8th Jäger Division and first saw action on the Eastern Front in Demjansk. He was promoted to *Generalleutnant* in September 1943.

Knight's Cross: Awarded on 26 March 1944 as *Generalleutnant* and Commander of the 8th *Jäger* Division for his actions and leadership during the fighting on the northern sector of the Soviet front at Demjansk and Lake Ilmen and during the retreat from Leningrad. In March 1944 his division was ordered to the southern sector and saw action during the retreats through Ukraine and the Carpathians. From 25 October Volckamer von Kirchensittenbach took over the command of the L. Army Corps as part of Army Group North, seeing action in the area around North Courland, and he was promoted to the rank of *General der Gebirgstruppe* in January 1945. From 10 April until the end of the war he was also given the leadership of the 16th Army, seeing action in the Courland Pocket, where his command was surrounded by Soviet forces. He surrendered to Soviet forces on 9 May and in February 1949 he was sentenced to twenty-five years' imprisonment by a Military Tribunal in Pskov. He was released and repatriated to Germany on 8 October 1955.

Dr Phil. Hans SPEIDEL

Generalleutnant

* 28 October 1897, Metzingen, Urach
\+ 28 November 1984, Bad Honnef

Knight's Cross: Awarded on 1 April 1944 as *Generalleutnant* and Chief of the General Staff of the 8th Army for his leadership and services to the Commander-

Hans Speidel joined the Army in November 1914 and served as a company leader at the Battle of Somme in 1916 before being appointed a battalion adjutant. He ended the war as a regimental adjutant with the rank of *Leutnant* and remained in the Army after the war, having been awarded both classes of the Iron Cross. In February 1925 he achieved a doctorate in politics and four years later he trained as a Staff Officer and was assigned to the Defence Ministry in Berlin. By 1936 he had been promoted to *Major* and was serving as company commander with Infantry Regiment 56 in Ulm. At the beginning of the war in September 1939 he served as Chief of Operations on the 33rd Infantry Division and later he became Chief of Operations of the IX. Army Corps. He was promoted to *Oberst* in February 1941 while serving as Chief of the General Staff of the Military Commander of France, General der Infanterie Carl-Heinrich von Stülpnagel.

After the war Speidel served for some time as professor of modern history at Tübingen and in 1950 published his book *Invasion 1944: Rommel and the Normandy Campaign* before being involved in both the development and creation of the new German Army, which he joined, reaching the rank of full *general*. He was subsequently appointed Supreme Commander of the Allied NATO ground forces in Central Europe in April 1957, a command that he held until retirement in September 1963.

in-Chief of the 8th Army, *General der Infanterie* Otto Wöhler, on the Eastern Front. Speidel did not agree with Hitler's and the Nazis' policies against the Jews and was involved in the July 1944 plot to kill the dictator. On 1 July 1944, when he was Chief of the General Staff of Army Group B, he confided in *Generalfeldmarschall* Erwin Rommel, who counted on his full support but never really received any conformation regarding this. Following the assassination attempt on Hitler on 20 July 1944 at Rastenburg, the Gestapo rounded up almost 5,000 Germans and tortured and executed many, which included high-ranking officers. Speidel was arrested by the Gestapo on 7 September and later appeared before an Army Court of Honour. *Generalfeldmarschall* Gerd von Rundstedt, *Generaloberst* Heinz Guderian and even *Generalfeldmarschall* Wilhelm Keitel refused to expel Speidel from the Army, so he wasn't required to appear before the People's Court, which would have meant a death sentence. He was sentenced to seven months in prison by the Gestapo and as Allied forces approached the location where he was being held he managed to slip away from his captors and went into hiding. On 29 April 1945 he gave himself up to French troops who had entered the area and was released from prison soon after the end of the war. After the war, Speidel served for a time as professor of modern history and later published a book: *Invasion 1944: Rommel and the Normandy Campaign*, before being involved in both the development and creation of the new German Army.

Egon Cäsar Waldemar Georg von NEINDORFF

Generalleutnant

* 12 September 1892, Coblenz
+ 15 April 1944, Sagrobelje near Ternopol

Knight's Cross: Awarded on 4 April 1944 as *Generalmajor* and Battle Commandant of Ternopol while attached to the 4th Army for his leadership

Egon von Neindorff entered the Army with the 1st Company of Jäger Battalion 12, Freiburg in March 1911 and saw action with this unit at the start of the First World War. He was later promoted to *Oberleutnant* and served as a platoon leader and later as company leader, remaining with the Army after the war. He served in Leipzig as an infantry commander and later as an intelligence officer, and was promoted to *Oberstleutnant* in October 1936. He saw action in the Second World War as commander of Infantry Regiment 456 and from November 1940 he was commander of Infantry Regiment 433, seeing action in the Balkans, and was wounded in mid-1942. From September he was commander of the 289th Infantry Division in France and later, in May 1943, he was appointed commander of the 356th Infantry Division and promoted to *Generalmajor* in December 1943.

and defensive action. At Ternopol his men, who had become encircled on 23 March 1944, fought a desperate defensive action, which saw them repel a far superior Soviet force. Neindorff and his men concentrated on tying down significant Soviet forces and this played a major role in assisting the XXXXVIII. Army Corps, which had been tied down by a strong Soviet force. Hitler had declared Ternopol a fortress to be held until the last man, and it was.

Knight's Cross with Oakleaves: Awarded posthumously to become the 457th recipient on 17 April 1944 as *Generalmajor* and Battle Commandant of Tarnopol, which he held for a total of twenty-four days and faithfully fulfilled Hitler's orders. The Red Army surrounded the city, killing almost all the German defenders and reducing Ternopol to ruins. Neindorff was killed by a bomb during the attempted breakout from the city on 15 April 1944, and together with the Knight's Cross he was posthumously promoted to the rank of *Generalleutnant*.

Gerhard Ernst Ludwig MATZKY

General der Infanterie

* 19 March 1894, Küstrin
+ 9 June 1983, Bad Godesberg

Knight's Cross: Awarded on 5 April 1944 as *Generalleutnant* and Commander of the 21st Infantry Division for actions during the fighting in the Soviet Union and in the retreat from Leningrad. From 28 March until 28 May 1944

Gerhard Matzky entered the Army in March 1912 with the Upper Silesian Infantry Regiment Nr. 63 and was commissioned as a *Leutnant* the following year. He served in the First World War as a platoon leader, an ordnance officer and company leader. He was wounded three times and remained in the Army after the war. He was later attached to the War Ministry and from 1926 served as adjutant to *Oberst* Werner von Fritsch, then later Chief of Staff to *Oberst* Gerd von Rundstedt. In April 1934 he served as operations officer with Military District Command VII in Munich and from September 1938 he served as military attaché in the German Embassy in Tokyo with the rank of *Oberst*. In January 1941 he served as quartermaster on the General Staff of the Army and from January 1943 he was commander of the 21st Infantry Division.

Matzky served as temporary Leader of the XXVIII. Army Corps and saw action near Lyuban and Pskov in the Soviet Union. From May he was briefly Commander of the 21st Infantry Division as part of Army Group North. In July he took command of the XXVI. Army Corps and was promoted to *General der Infanterie* in September, seeing action in East Prussia as part of the 4th Army. Together with the XXVII. Army Corps, his corps fought with Soviet forces south of Gusev in the Soviet Union, where enemy forces broke through for a time but the situation was soon restored through counter-attacks. The Battle of East Prussia began soon after and his corps and the 3rd Panzer Army were soon in combat with Soviet forces. After a few days the Soviets broke through and the Germans were forced to retreat. In mid-April Matzky was appointed commander of Fortress Pilau as well as the troops from his corps, which was pushed back by enemy forces and had to retreat. In May 1945, after leading his men to Schleswig-Holstein in Germany, he surrendered his troops to British forces and was imprisoned until February 1948.

Adam Detlof Konrad Hellmuth REYMANN

Generalleutnant

* 24 November 1892, Neustadt, Silesia
+ 8 December 1988, Garmisch-Partenkirchen, Bavaria

Knight's Cross: Awarded on 5 April 1944 as *Generalleutnant* and Commander of the 13th *Luftwaffe* Field Division for his outstanding leadership during the

Hellmuth Reymann served as a platoon leader with the 9th Company of Infantry Regiment 62 during the first years of the First World War and was awarded the Iron Cross 1st and 2nd Classes. Promoted to *Oberleutnant* in 1917, he later served as deputy adjutant on the staff of the 24th Infantry Brigade and ended the war as a battalion leader. In August 1935 he transferred into the *Luftwaffe*, however just two months later he joined the Army and was attached to the War Ministry until January 1936, when he was appointed tactics instructor at the War School in Dresden. From November 1939, with the rank of *Oberst*, he was appointed commander of Infantry Regiment 205. He saw action during the invasion of France from May 1940, and later during the invasion of the Soviet Union. From September 1942, after almost eight months in the Reserves after suffering from dysentery, he took over command of the 254th Infantry Division while seeing action in the Soviet Union. Promoted to *Generalmajor*, in October he was transferred as commander of the 212th Infantry Division.

fighting in the Leningrad area during the German retreat from the region in early 1944. As his division pulled back through Sapolje in Kaliningrad, Reymann demonstrated great skill as a commander and he led his men during the fierce fighting south of St Petersburg, where his command suffered heavy losses. Towards the end of May 1944 he took command of the 11th East Prussian Infantry Division and continued to see action on the Eastern Front.

Reymann is seen here with *Oberleutnant* Egon von der Marwitz, who had been awarded the Knight's Cross on 12 August 1944, and on the right is his commanding officer, *Major* Heinz-Oskar Laebe, who had been awarded the Knight's Cross on 7 March 1944.

Knight's Cross with Oakleaves: He became the 672nd recipient on 28 November 1944 as *Generalleutnant* and Commander of the 11th Infantry Division for his excellent leadership on the Eastern Front. He saw action in the Battle of Tannenberg Line between 25 July and 10 August, where he took a major role in the pushing back of a large Soviet force. Later in October his command took part in the fierce fighting against a Soviet force that had penetrated the thick forests in the Courland area. On 16 December 1944 Reymann was personally decorated with the Oakleaves by *SS-Reichsführer* Heinrich Himmler at Trossingen, Württemberg. From 6 March 1945 he was named by Hitler as the new commander of the Military District of Berlin, succeeding *Generalleutnant* Bruno Ritter von Haunenschild. When he entered Berlin he soon found that there were no plans in place to evacuate the city, and he didn't agree with Hitler's plans to destroy Berlin's bridges. He believed that destroying the bridges would deprive Berlin of its electricity, water and fuel and when Hitler ordered their destruction in his so-called Nero Order, Reymann refused and met with *Reichsminister* Albert Speer, who also was against the order. However, on 22 April Reymann was relieved of his command of Berlin after Hitler had been convinced by Goebbels and Bormann that he was not up to the task. He later escaped the region of Berlin that faced Soviet forces and led almost 20,000 German soldiers to the American lines and surrendered to US and British troops on 7 May 1945. Reymann was a defence witness for *Generaloberst* Lothar Rendulic during his trial at Nuremberg.

Wilhelm Hermann BLECKWENN

Generalmajor/Konteradmiral

* 21 October 1906, Berge, Bersenbrück near Hannover
\+ 10 May 1989, Saarbrücken

Knight's Cross: Awarded on 6 April 1944 as *Oberst* and Commander of Grenadier Regiment 487, part of the 267th Infantry Division, for significantly aiding the 31st Infantry Division on 21 February 1944. On that day the Soviets pushed into the German lines, especially near the Dnieper bend, and Bleckwenn played a major role in ensuring the division was not destroyed.

Knight's Cross with Oakleaves: He became the 621st recipient on 18 October 1944 as *Oberst* and Commander of Grenadier Regiment 487, and also under his command at this time was a small battle group that broke through to East Prussia after forty-four days of fighting with the Soviets in Belorussia. On the

Wilhelm Bleckwenn entered the police in April 1925, where he remained until August 1935, when he transferred into the Army with the rank of *Oberleutnant*. Promoted to *Hauptmann* in October 1936, he was assigned to an officers' course at the Dresden War School in July 1938, before being transferred to Machine-gun Company 14. In January 1940 he was appointed commander of I. Battalion of Border Infantry Regiment 127 in East Prussia, and later, as part of the XXIV. Army Corps, he saw action during the Battle of France. On 22 November he took over as commander of the II. Battalion of Infantry Regiment 690 and remained in France on occupation duty, and then after a five-month stint at an officers' training course from March 1941, he was assigned as commander of III. Battalion of Infantry Regiment 256 and saw action at Bobruisk and Kiev as part of Army Group Centre. As part of the 267th Infantry Division, he saw action at Moscow, where the division suffered during the Soviet winter offensive and lost many horses due to the cold and lack of supplies.

night of 4–5 August, Bleckwenn and his men overcame the torrential currents of the Memel River while crossing it at a point south of Druskininkai. The Oakleaves were presented personally by *SS-Reichsführer* Heinrich Himmler on 7 November 1944 in Posen. On 28 February Bleckwenn succeeded *Konteradmiral* Hans Hartmann as Inspector of Infantry with the 1st Naval Infantry Division and at the same time he took command of the division, which suffered heavy losses during the fierce defensive fighting in the bridgehead between Alt Damm and Greifenhagen. On 1 March Bleckwenn transferred to the Kriegsmarine, according to an official telex from the Army High Command to the Navy High Command. Although it cannot be confirmed officially, some sources report that soon after he transferred he held the rank of *Konteradmiral*.

Otto Johann DRESCHER

Generalleutnant

* 5 October 1895, Nikl, Zwitau, Austro-Hungary
+ 13 August 1944, near Jacelli, Memel, East Prussia

Knight's Cross: Awarded on 6 April 1944 as *Generalleutnant* and Commander of the 267th Infantry Division while attached to the XII. Army Corps for his leadership and bravery for actions on Eastern Front and the Soviet Union. Between 21 and 29 February 1944 his division held the main thrust of the

Soviet offensive and prevented a major breakthrough in Mogilev, Belarus. Drescher was presented with the Knight's Cross personally by the Commanding General of the XII. Army Corps *General der Infanterie*, Kurt von Tippelskirch, on 13 April 1944. It was later noted that Drescher and his command saved the front line from being torn open a total of three times during this period and all through his own independent actions. On this occasion Drescher removed one of his grenadier regiments from the front line and dispatched it along with some artillery in such a way that contact with the neighbouring division was maintained. In July 1944 his division was encircled and smashed near Minsk, along with the bulk of the 4th Army, and remnants of the division were destroyed near Memel on 13 August, the same day that Drescher was killed.

Ludwig Heinrich 'Heinz' GAEDCKE

Generalmajor

* 16 January 1905, Gruden, Brandenburg
+ 22 December 1992, Waldesch, Rhineland-Palatinate

Knight's Cross: Awarded on 7 April 1944 as *Oberst im Generalstab* and Chief of the General Staff of the XI. Army Corps for actions on the Eastern Front. The award was presented by his commanding officer, *General der Infanterie* Rudolf von Bünau, and from July Gaedcke served as Acting Chief of the General Staff of the 4th Army under *General der Infanterie* Friedrich Hossbach. From 15 August 1944 he served as Chief of the General Staff of the 6th Army under *General der Artillerie* Maximilian Fretter-Pico, seeing action on the Eastern Front. After being virtually destroyed, the High Command re-established the remnants and it was deployed

Henrich Gaedcke entered the Army as a *Fahnenjunker* with Infantry Regiment 8 from August 1925 and was commissioned as a *Leutnant* two years later. From October 1935 he was attached to the War Ministry, now with the rank of *Hauptmann*, and two years later he was attached to the Operations Department of the Army General Staff. In June 1940 he was appointed Chief of Operations in the General Staff of 25th Infantry Division at the time of the invasion of France. He was promoted to *Major* in October 1940 and the following month his command was motorised and saw action on the Eastern Front.

in defence of Transylvania. From October Gaedcke led his command in heavy defensive battles in eastern Hungary and fought between the rivers Tisza and Danube until the end of 1944. In November he was promoted to *Generalmajor* and by the end of December he was involved in heavy battles between Lake Balaton and the Danube. Later the 6th Army were involved in the defence of Budapest and by March 1945 he saw action in the Székesfehérvár area of Hungary and then south of the Danube to the Eastern Alps. He went into Allied captivity from 9 May 1945, being released in November 1947. He later rejoined the armed forces and by April 1961 had been promoted to the rank of *Generalleutnant* in the *Bundeswehr*.

Vincenz MÜLLER

Generalleutnant

* 5 November 1894, Aichach, Bavaria
+ 12 May 1961, Berlin

Knight's Cross: Awarded on 7 April 1944 as *Generalleutnant* and Commander of the XXVII. Army Corps for his leadership during heavy fighting near Nevel in the north-western Soviet Union and near Belarus. From 5 to 30 June he briefly commanded the XII. Army Corps before taking over as Commanding General of the 4th Army on 1 July 1944. He took part in the heavy fighting near Minsk and was reported as missing, and it was later reported that he had been captured by the Soviets four days later. During captivity he joined the National Committee for the Liberation of Germany and the League of German Officers. He was released from prison in 1948 and became Chief Inspector of the *Volkspolizei* in East Germany, and he also joined the National German Democratic Party and was elected Vice-Chairman from 1949 until 1952. He later joined the National People's Army as a *Generalleutnant* and took various postings, including one with the department of the interior. He retired in 1958 and in May 1961 he died after falling from his balcony. From earlier nervous breakdowns and health problems it was assumed he had committed suicide.

Günther KRAPPE

Generalleutnant

* 13 April 1893, Schilde, Dramburg
+ 31 December 1983, Altena, Westfalen

Knight's Cross: Awarded on 11 April 1944 as *Generalleutnant* and Commander of the 61st Infantry Division for his actions during the retreat through the Baltic States, where he and his division distinguished itself in the fighting near Narva, Estonia. He saw more fighting in Belarus around the area of the Daugava River area and then in the town of Sigula in Latvia. In October the German retreat began and his command took part in defence fighting while retreating and in December the division was withdrawn to be refreshed, later being renamed the 61st *Volksgrenadier* Division. Krappe was transferred to the Reserves and in November he took a course for commanding generals. From February 1945 he was given the temporary leadership of the X. SS Army Corps until he was taken prisoner by the Soviets on 6 March. He was kept in a Soviet prison until March 1949.

Günther Krappe entered Army service as a *Fahnenjunker* with Fusilier Regiment 34 from September 1912 and was commissioned as a *Leutnant* in March 1914. He served during the First World War as a platoon and company leader, rising to the rank of *Oberleutnant* in May 1917. He remained with the Army after the war and served as a company commander and intelligence officer with the 2nd Division, and from October 1935 he served as a battalion commander with Infantry Regiment 59. He was promoted to *Oberst* in April 1939 and later served as military attaché in Budapest and later in Madrid. From February 1943 he took over the leadership of the 61st Infantry Division, with the rank of *Generalmajor*.

Siegfried Karl Peter Franz RASP

General der Infanterie

* 10 January 1898, Munich
+ 2 September 1968, Murnau

Knight's Cross: Awarded on 15 April 1944 as *Generalmajor* and Commander of the 335th Infantry Division for actions in Nikopol in Ukraine against a strong

Soviet force. He received various assessments with regard to his command from various senior commanders including *Generaloberst* Karl-Adolf Hollidt, who was one of the senior commanders that recommended Rasp for the Knight's Cross. He said Rasp 'was brave tough and agile and led his division with a lot of momentum and empathy, he has always been an excellent commander'. Rasp later saw action in Mykolaiv and Kishinev, part of Ukraine, when his division was down to only around 2,500 men and he took part in battles on the Dnieper bend and in Zaporozhye. Promoted to *Generalleutnant* in April, in June he was attached to the General Staff of the Commander-in-Chief West *Generalfeldmarschall* Gerd von Rundstedt. From mid-July to the end of August 1944 he was briefly commander of the 543rd Grenadier Division and then took command of the 78th Grenadier Division. He was promoted to *General der Infanterie* in December 1944 and was appointed Commander of the 19th Army, taking over from *General der Infanterie* Friedrich Wiese on the Western Front. His last command of the war was that of Army Corps XXXI., also known as Army Corps Ems. It was a brief command as he surrendered eleven days later on 5 May to British troops in Wesermünde near Hannover. Rasp was appointed by the Allied authorities the Commander of all German prisoners at the Allied Prisoner-of-War Camp at Münster from 19 September 1945 until 26 February 1948.

Siegfried Rasp entered the Army in September 1915 and was commissioned as a *Leutnant* the following year, serving as a battalion adjutant in January 1917. He served as a Staff Officer throughout the First World War and remained in the Army after the war, rising to the rank of *Hauptmann* in February 1933. He served as an instructor with the War Academy from July 1934 and from November 1938, and now with the rank of *Major*, he served as Chief of Operations of the 17th Infantry Division. He later served as Chief of Operations of the 1st Army from October 1939 and from January 1940 he served as tactics instructor at the General Staff Officers' School in Dresden. From June he was Chief of Operations of the 7th Army, now with the rank of *Oberstleutnant*. He later served as Chief of the General Staff of the XXII. Army Corps and from late 1943 took command of the 335th Infantry Division, now with the rank of *Generalmajor*.

Hinrich Friedrich WARRELMANN

Generalmajor

* 26 April 1904, Rüdershausen-Strückhausen, Oldenburg
+ 9 October 1980, Westerkappeln, North Rhine-Westphalia

Knight's Cross: Awarded on 16 April 1944 as *Oberst* and Commander of Grenadier Regiment 502, part of the 290th Infantry Division, in recognition of his outstanding combat performance during the tough defensive battles south of Newel, in the winter of 1943–44. On 21 January 1944 Warrelmann put together a scratch unit in order to make a counter-attack on a Soviet force, and he had assembled men from his regimental headquarters and made the attack south of Ilyushin, which had been a success.

Knight's Cross with Oakleaves: Awarded on 19 August 1944 to become the 555th recipient as *Oberst* and Commander of Grenadier Regiment 502 for his continued leadership and personal courage during the defensive fighting east of Daugavpils in Latvia against troops of the Red Army. In November 1944 he attended the 16th Divisional Leaders' Course at Hirschberg before returning to front-line action in January 1945, as deputy commander of the 272nd *Volksgrenadier* Division during its recovery after heavy fighting in the Eifel campaign. On 25 February he took command of the 183rd *Volksgrenadier* Division on the Western Front while fighting troops from the US 9th Army. As a result it wasn't long before his command was cut off in the Ruhr Pocket area and surrounded by American troops, and on 15 April he surrendered his command. He was promoted to *Generalmajor* on 20 April, while in captivity, and he remained a prisoner of the Americans until his release in 1947, when he returned to Germany.

Hinrich Warrelmann entered the Army in October 1921 and was attached to the 11th Company of Infantry Regiment 16 in Oldenburg. By July 1934, now an *Oberleutnant*, he was a company commander in Hannover and by the start of the Second World War he was commander of the 12th Machine-gun Company of Infantry Regiment 37. He saw action during the Polish campaign and in France, where he won both classes of the Iron Cross as *Hauptmann* and battalion commander. From May 1941 he was a tactics instructor at the Army Flying School in Weimar-Nohra and later served as commander of Machine-Gun Battalion 2, now with the rank of *Major*. In April 1942 he was commander of III. Battalion of Rifle Regiment 115, wounded in North Africa and awarded the German Cross in Gold.

Werner Arthur Otto FRIEBE

Generalmajor

* 12 July 1897, Droschkau, Upper Silesia
+ 8 March 1962, Stuttgart, Baden-Württemberg

Knight's Cross: Awarded on 21 April 1944 as *Oberst* and Leader of the 8th Panzer Division for his leadership of Panzer Formation *Friebe* an ad hoc unit that Friebe commanded between 21 March and 18 April 1944 in the Soviet Union. He continued to command the 8th Panzer Division and helped to free the trapped 361st Infantry Division near Brody. He was credited with destroying or capturing enemy equipment that included 168 enemy tanks, 187 artillery pieces, 142 anti-tank guns, 540 mines, and taking 530 prisoners. As result of his success he was promoted to the rank of *Generalmajor*, however things were about to change. On 15 July 1944, during operations along the Bug River, Friebe deviated from his orders and decided to make up time. Instead of moving slowly at night he decided to move his entire divisions along main roads during daylight. As a result his troops were attacked by Soviet fighters and suffered heavy casualties. Friebe lost 4,545 men out of 4,600. It was a massacre! *General der Panzertruppe* Helmut Balck, the Commanding General of the XXXXVIII. Panzer Corps, was furious when he found out and relieved Friebe of his command. He was not re-employed until September, when he was made Chief of the General Staff of Military District III in Berlin, a major demotion. On 8 May 1945 Friebe was taken prisoner by American troops, escaping Soviet capture, and was imprisoned until May 1948, when he was released.

Werner Freibe was a war volunteer and joined the battalion of Fusilier Regiment 38 in September 1914, being commissioned as a *Leutnant* in March 1916. He attended various training courses before being appointed leader of the signals battalion for his regiment and ended the war his regiment's signals officer. He remained with the Army after the war, serving with Infantry Regiment 7 and Pioneer Battalion 3, and was promoted to *Hauptmann* in September 1933. He was attached to the Troop Office from May 1934 and was promoted to *Major* in March 1937. Later that year took command of the 1st Company of Motorcycle Rifle Battalion 3. By the beginning of the war he held the rank of *Oberstleutnant* and served as Chief of Operations of the 20th Motorised Infantry Division, and from January 1941 he served as Chief of the General Staff of XXXXVIII. Motorized Army Corps. This later became a Panzer Corps, serving in the Soviet Union.

Carl Ulrich Ernst Paul ANDERS

Generalmajor

* 31 August 1893 in Günz, Pomerania off the Baltic Coast
+ 28 January 1972, Prien am Chiemsee in Bavaria

Knight's Cross: Awarded on 4 May 1944 as *Oberst* and Commander of Grenadier Regiment 484, part of the 254th Infantry Division, LIX. Army Corps, in recognition of his leadership during the fierce fighting around the area of the Battle of Kamianets–Podilskyi Pocket in western Ukraine in late March 1944. The Soviets succeeded in creating a pocket in which they trapped almost 220,000 German soldiers but by mid-April the Germans had managed to fight their way out and with relief forces led by the 2nd SS-Panzer Corps, the majority of the 1st Panzer Army were rescued. In September 1944 Anders was delegated with the temporary leadership of the 168th Infantry Division and took over the leadership of the 88th Infantry Division on 31 December. On 30 January 1945, he was promoted to *Generalmajor* and appointed Commander of the Infantry Division, briefly seeing action in Baranów, Poland, as part of the XXXXII. Army Corps. Captured a few days later when his division surrendered to Soviet troops, he was later convicted as a war criminal by a Soviet court and eventually released on 28 October 1955.

Carl Anders joined the Army as a *Fahnenjunker* with Infantry Regiment 42 in April 1912 and was commissioned as a *Leutnant* in August 1913. At the beginning of the First World War he was appointed platoon leader and from February 1915 was company leader in Infantry Regiment 152. Promoted to *Oberleutnant* in October 1916, he was seriously wounded in May 1917 and spent six months recovering in hospital. During the last months of war he served as adjutant with Infantry Regiment 152, and finally ordnance officer of 41st Infantry Division. In May 1940 *Oberstleutnant* Anders took part in the invasion of France, and later as battalion commander with Infantry Regiment 581 during the attack on the Soviet Union in June 1941. He took over as commander of the Infantry Regiment 484 from early January until June 1942 and saw action at the Volkhov Pocket, and then towards Novgorod. He was promoted to *Oberst* two months later.

Adolf FISCHER

Generalmajor

* 23 July 1893, Schwerte, Westphalia
+ 23 October 1947, Belgrade, Yugoslavia

Knight's Cross: Awarded on 4 May 1944 as *Oberst* and Commander of Grenadier Regiment 459 and Acting Commander of the 96th Infantry Division for action in the Kamenets–Podolsky Pocket in the Soviet Union. At this time the Soviets successfully created a pocket trapping about 220,000 German soldiers of the 1st Panzer Army that was under the direction of *Generaloberst* Hans Hube and *Generalfeldmarschall* Erich von Manstein. Most of the German panzer army was rescued but it came at a cost as they had to leave almost all of their heavy equipment. Fischer later took command of the 367th Infantry Division and was promoted to *Generalmajor* in July 1944, seeing action in East Prussia. In August he was appointed leader of the Formation Staff of Infantry Division *Rhön*, which existed only until 26 August 1944, when it was redesignated the 566th *Volksgrenadier* Division. He then took command of Battle Group South East and was taken prisoner at the end of the war by troops from Yugoslavia. He was later condemned to death as a war criminal, being executed by firing squad on 23 October 1947.

Adolf Fischer entered the Army as a war volunteer with Infantry Regiment 15 in August 1914 and was commissioned as a *Leutnant* in March 1915. He later served as a company officer with Landwehr Infantry Regiment 110 and served as a temporary adjutant and then company leader from September 1917. He left the Army in 1920 and joined the police in Münster, rising to the rank of *Polizei-Major* in September 1935. The following month he transferred back into the Army and served as battalion commander with Infantry Regiment 80 with the rank of *Major*. In June 1940, now with the rank of *Oberstleutnant*, he was appointed commander of Infantry Regiment 459, part of the 251st Infantry Division, and saw action during the invasion of France and later in the Soviet Union.

Carl-Erik KOEHLER

General der Kavallerie

* 3 December 1895, Mannheim
+ 8 December 1958, Eppensen, Melzen

Knight's Cross: Awarded on 4 May 1944 as *Generalleutnant* and Commander of the 306th Infantry Division for actions in the area of the Dnieper bend withdrawal and in the retreat into Bessarabia on the Eastern Front. In August he was appointed commander of Central Norway, where he took command of the XXXIII. Army Corps and saw action in and around Trondheim. He was promoted to *General der Kavallerie* in November 1944 and took over command of the XX. Army Corps from 16 April 1945. He was attached to the 12th Army in the area near Magdeburg and was tasked with advancing on Potsdam in order to relieve the besieged city of Berlin. His command was ordered to attack and relieve Potsdam on the night of 26 April but this was unsuccessful and by 1 May German troops began to withdraw from the area. Without a strong Soviet pursuit, Koehler's troops marched into Tangermünde on the Elbe River in Germany, where they surrendered to the Western Allies.

Carl-Erik Koehler joined the Army as a war volunteer in August 1914, serving with Dragon Regiment 24, and commissioned as a *Leutnant* in November 1915. He was appointed adjutant a year later. From October 1930 he was attached to the staff of the Commandant of Berlin and was then attached to the War Ministry with the rank of *Hauptmann*. In October 1935 he was Chief of Operations on the Staff of the 4th Division and from February 1940 he served as Chief of Staff to the General Army Office. In March 1943, now with the rank of *Generalmajor*, he was appointed commander of the 306th Infantry Division, seeing action in the Soviet Union. From 8 April 1944 he was acting commandant of Fortress Crete while *Generalleutnant* Bruno Bräuer was on leave.

Hans Friedrich Max PIEKENBROCK

Generalleutnant

* 3 October 1893, Essen, Rhine Province
+ 16 December 1959, Porz-Cologne, North Rhine-Westphalia

Knight's Cross: Awarded on 4 May 1944 as *Generalmajor* and Commander of the 208th Infantry Division for his command of his division during the heavy fighting near Kamianets-Podilskyi in western Ukraine between late 1943 and April 1944. He was promoted to *Generalleutnant* in March 1944 and later saw action at Ternopol in Ukraine and then in the Hube Pocket against a strong Soviet force. On 30 March 1945 he took over the leadership of the LIX. Army Corps and while fighting Soviet forces in Czechoslovakia he surrendered his command on 12 May 1945. He was sent to a prison in Butyrskaya near Moscow before being transferred to Prison No. 2, Vladimir, and then to the NKVD Camp No. 48, in Černcy, Ležnovo. There he was condemned by a Military Court to twenty-five years' hard labour but was released on a general amnesty in October 1955.

Hans Piekenbrock entered the Army in September 1914 as a volunteer and served as an ordnance officer and as a signals officer with the rank of *Leutnant*. He remained in the Army after the war, serving with Mounted Regiment 15 and later with a cavalry division. From October 1934 he served as Chief of Operations of the 18th Infantry Division, now with the rank of *Major*. From July 1936 he was Chief of Department 1 in the Reich War Ministry responsible for Foreign Espionage and Intelligence. He attended a divisional leaders' course in March 1943 and was appointed commander of the 208th Infantry Division in June 1943, being promoted to *Generalmajor* two months later.

Max Severus Hermann Carl-August von SCHÖNFELD

Generalmajor

* 4 September 1898, Schönebeck, Calbe
+ 16 April 1944, Ternopol, Soviet Union

Knight's Cross: Awarded on 4 May 1944 as *Oberst* and Commander of Grenadier Regiment 949 while attached to the 359th Infantry Division, which was sent to the Soviet Union in early 1944 and saw action on southern part of the front as part of the 4th Panzer Army. Schönfeld led his regiment during fierce fighting west of Ternopol against heavy Soviet attacks in April. He was promoted to *Generalmajor* on 1 April 1944 and two weeks later he was killed in action in Ternopol. He has no grave.

Hans Harald TRÖGER

Generalleutnant

* 29 August 1896, Plauen
+ 21 January 1982, Schwanau, Ortenaukreis

Knight's Cross: Awarded on 4 May 1944 as *Generalmajor* and Commander of the 25th Panzer Division while attached to the 1st Panzer Army for actions during the withdrawal across northern Ukraine in March 1944. The following month his division was sent to Aalborg in Denmark to be rebuilt and receive much-

Hans Tröger entered the Army in July 1915 and saw action with Pioneer Battalion 9 from October. He was commissioned as a *Leutnant* the following year. From February 1917 he served as supply officer with the IX. Army Corps and was awarded both classes of the Iron Cross. He stayed in the Army after the war, rising to the rank of *Hauptmann* in May 1933 and took command of Reconnaissance Battalion 3 from October 1934. Three years later he was attached to the War Ministry in Berlin and at the start of the Second World War he commanded a motorcycle battalion as part of the 3rd Panzer Division. He later served with the 14th Panzer Division and was promoted to *Oberst* in March 1942. From December he commanded the 27th Panzer Division, rising to the rank of *Generalleutnant* in April 1944.

needed reinforcements, and at the same time Tröger was promoted to the rank of *Generalleutnant*. On 25 May Tröger was transferred to take over command of the 13th Panzer Division while attached to Army Group South Ukraine and his orders were to stop the Soviets from capturing the Romanian oil fields. From July 1944 his command received modern equipment, which included the *Panther G* tank and the *Jagdpanzer IV*. However, during the August Red Army offensive his command suffered heavy losses. In September his division took part in the fighting around Kishinev, the capital of Moldova, and was soon cut off. Tröger led part of his command in an attempted breakout, however his attempt failed with him and his men being captured by Bulgarian troops and later handed over to the Soviets, who imprisoned him until October 1955.

Walter Karl Otto DENKERT

Generalleutnant

* 23 February 1897, Kiel, Schleswig-Holstein
+ 9 July 1982, Kiel, Schleswig-Holstein

Knight's Cross: Awarded on 14 May 1944 as *Oberst* and Deputy Commander of the 19th Panzer Division while attached to the 1st Panzer Army for actions near Ukraine on the Eastern Front. He led his troops during a heavy snow storm against Soviet forces and succeeded in breaking through the strong anti-tankgun positions. His forces succeeded in capturing the forest and village nearby, which was of great importance for the protection of the northern flank from Soviet forces, and from this position his forces were

Walter Denkert entered the Army in August 1914 as a war volunteer with Infantry Regiment 84 and first saw action in November with Infantry Regiment 23, being commissioned as a *Leutnant* in May 1915. He later served at the front with Infantry Regiment 379 until he was wounded in March 1918, and after the war he entered the police, rising to the rank of *Polizei-Major* in November 1934. He re-entered the Army in October 1935 as battalion commander with Infantry Regiment 65 and was promoted to *Oberstleutnant* in March 1939. From August that year he was battalion commander with Infantry Regiment 271. From April 1941 he served on the Staff of the General of Infantry as a specialist for anti-aircraft units and later served with Infantry Regiment 47 while attached to the 22nd Infantry Air Landing Division.

able to destroy many Soviet tanks. Promoted to *Generalmajor* in June 1944, he took command of the 3rd Panzer Grenadier Division in October, seeing action near Metz, and then took part in the Battle of Aachen. From January 1945 he led his division into the area around Lichtenborn in Germany and later his command helped with the defence of Gemünd in the Eifel region. He then led his division during the withdrawal to the southern edge of Cologne and from mid-March his division led a counter-attack on the northern edge of the US bridgehead near Remagen. Promoted to *Generalleutnant* in April, he later led his division during the attempt by Army Group G to break out of the Ruhr Pocket, but this failed and his division moved to the Ruhr area, where he surrendered to the Allies.

Wolfgang Max LANGE

Generalleutnant

* 1 June 1898, Tübingen
+ 10 February 1988, Gilching, Munich

Wolfgang Lange entered Army service as a *Fahnenjunker* in April 1915 with Infantry Regiment 126, seeing action during the First World War until he was captured by French forces in December 1916. He stayed in the Army after the war and by July 1936 had been promoted to *Major* and was Chief of Operations on the Staff of the 34th Division. In August 1940, now with the rank of *Oberstleutnant*, Lange saw action during the invasion of France while serving on the General Staff of the XXXVIII. Army Corps. He later served as Chief of Staff of Army Control Inspector in France, helping with the French Armistice in central and southern France. Now with the rank of *Generalmajor*, he took command of the 145th Infantry Regiment from July 1942 and later saw action as commander of Infantry Regiment 980.

Knight's Cross: Awarded on 14 May 1944 as *Generalmajor* and Commander of Corps Battalion C while attached to the XIII. Army Corps for actions near Vinnitsa in western Ukraine. Promoted to *Generalleutnant* in July, a month later he took command of the 564th *Volksgrenadier* Division, which had been put together during troop manoeuvres in Döllersheim, Austria, and most of its men ended up in the Ruhr Pocket. On 15 September Lange took command of the 183rd *Volksgrenadier* Division and saw action on the Western Front, where it suffered heavy losses in the battles of the Siegfried Line and at Aachen. A few months later his command faced the US 9th Army, where his 330th Grenadier regiment was virtually annihilated. Lange fought hard against a strong enemy and on 15 April he surrendered his command to the Americans in the area of the Ruhr Pocket.

Alfred August Nikolaus PHILIPPI

Generalmajor

* 3 August 1903, Bübingen, Saarbrücken
+ 15 June 1994, Winnweiler

Knight's Cross: Awarded on 14 May 1944 as *Oberst* and Commander of Grenadier Regiment 535 while attached to the 384th Infantry Division for his tactical skill and leadership during the retreating battles across the Bug River on the southern sector of the Eastern Front in early 1944. He transferred into the Reserves from July 1944 and in early August

Alfred Philippi entered the Army with Infantry Regiment 13 in April 1924 and was attached to the 8th Machine-Gun Company from December. He was commissioned as a *Leutnant* in August 1928, serving with Infantry Regiment 11 for the next seven years. From October 1935 he served as company commander with the 53rd and later 73rd Infantry Regiments with the rank of *Hauptmann*. At the start of the Second World War he served as adjutant of Infantry Regiment 73 in Hannover, and later attended various courses. From May 1942 Philippi served as Chief of Operations on the General Staff of the 111th Infantry Division, now with the rank of *Oberstleutnant*. He later served in a similar position with the 306th Infantry Division with the rank of *Oberst*, and from March 1943 he was commander of Grenadier Regiment 535.

he attended the 13th Divisional Leaders' Course in Hirschberg. On 2 September he took the brief leadership of the 569th *Volksgrenadier* Division and four days later he transferred as leader of the 361st *Volksgrenadier* Division. He saw action during the battles in Arnhem in the Netherlands before being transferred to the Saar sector, and after fighting in eastern France his division was posted to the Vosges Mountains. Philippi was promoted to *Generalmajor* on 1 January 1945 and his command was absorbed by the 559th *Volksgrenadier* Division in March. He was captured by British forces in May 1945 and was then handed over to the Americans, who kept him in prison until mid-1947.

Carl Gustav Rulemann WAGENER

Generalmajor

* 23 December 1901, Stanowitz, Schweidnitz
+ 3 June 1988, Hannover

Knight's Cross: Awarded on 14 May 1944 as *Oberst im Generalstab* and Chief of the General Staff of the 1st Panzer Army for his part in the defensive battles in southern Ukraine against the Red Army while under the command of *Generaloberst* Hans Hube. He then took part in the fighting in the Nikopol Bridgehead area and north of Kryvyi Rih in Ukraine, and in October he was promoted to *Generalmajor*. In November he was appointed Chief of the General Staff of the 5th Panzer Army under the command of *General der Panzertruppe* Hasso von Manteuffel and later took part in the Battle of Bulge in the Ardennes

Carl Wagener entered the Army in October 1921 and was commissioned as a *Leutnant* in December 1924, being attached to Mounted Regiment 11 in Neustadt from May 1925. From October 1934 he was attached to the War Academy in Berlin and from October 1935 was attached to the III. Army Corps, now with the rank of *Rittmeister*. He was a staff officer serving with the 9th Panzer Division at the outbreak of the Second World War and from January 1940 he served as tactics instructor at the War Academy. From July he was appointed Chief of Operations on the General Staff of the 10th Infantry Division, now with the rank of *Major*. From February 1941 he was Chief of Operations on the General Staff of the 3rd Panzer Group and from June 1941 saw action in the Soviet Union. From June 1942 he held a similar position with XXXX. Army Corps, which later became a Panzer Corps, now with the rank of *Oberstleutnant*.

region against US troops. From 20 February 1945, with the Ardennes Offensive over, Wagener was appointed Chief of the General Staff of Army Group B, seeing action in the Ruhr Pocket under the command of *Generalfeldmarschall* Walter Model. In mid-April 1945 Wagener took part in surrender negotiations with the US Airborne Corps under General Matthew Ridgway on behalf of *Generalfeldmarschall* Model. The negotiations did not go the way the Germans wanted and after a failed attempt to break out Wagener and his staff were taken prisoner by the Americans. He was released on 15 September 1947. Model, however, had gone missing and had in fact shot himself in a forest between Duisburg and the village of Lintorf on 21 April 1945.

Friedrich Edgar RÖHRICHT

General der Infanterie

* 16 June 1892, Liebau, Landeshut
+ 11 February 1967, Linz

Knight's Cross: Awarded on 15 May 1944 as *Generalleutnant* and Commander of the 95th Infantry Division, part of Army Group Centre, during the withdrawal in Rzhev on the Eastern Front. He later led his command as part of the 4th Army at Gomel and west of Smolensk in the summer fighting of 1943, and suffered heavy losses in the Bryansk attack that summer. By the time he had received his award he had been given the leadership of the LIX. Army Corps from March 1944, seeing action in the Soviet Union. He took part in the heavy fighting during the Soviet offensive around Kamianets-Podilskyi in western Ukraine and shortly after the German front stabilised for next few weeks. In mid-July 1944 his command was attacked by the Soviets and his command had to withdraw with the rest of the 1st Panzer Army. By the end of August his corps had to retreat further back to the Vistula at Nowy Korczyn, Tarnów in Poland, where it remained for the next few months. Röhricht was promoted to *General der Infanterie* in September 1944, and by January 1945, due to the Soviet winter offensive, his corps was pushed further back into the Moravian–Silesian area. Röhricht was relieved of his command on 26 January and entered the Reserves. He was taken prisoner by US troops in April 1945 in Altefeld, Thuringia. The following year he was sent to Special Camp No. 1 and then was transferred to London before being released towards the end of 1947.

Friedrich Joachim FANGOHR

General der Infanterie

* 12 August 1899, Hannover
+ 17 April 1956, Munich, Bavaria

Knight's Cross: Awarded on 9 June 1944 as *Generalleutnant* and Chief of the General Staff of Panzer Army Headquarters 4 for his organisation and operational contributions to the leadership of the 4th Panzer Army in the Soviet Union. He was one of a very few staff officers to be awarded the Knight's Cross and the German Cross in Gold for his service on the Eastern Front. On 23 August he was appointed commander of the 122nd Infantry Division and took part in the retreat through Estonia. His command was cut off in the Courland Pocket in western Latvia from October. However, Fangohr was transferred out in March 1945 and promoted to *General der Infanterie*, taking over as Commanding General of the I. Army Corps, then seeing action in the Courland area. On 9 May 1945 he was appointed Chief of the German Liaison Staff to the Headquarters of Allied Forces in Reims, taking part in the peace negotiations. He finally went into Allied captivity on 24 May 1945 and was interned until his release in March 1948.

Friedrich Fangohr entered the Army with Infantry Regiment 129 in December 1916 and after various courses he was commissioned as a *Leutnant* in November 1917. During the last months of the First World War he served as a platoon leader, a battalion adjutant and an orderly officer, all while attached to Infantry Regiment 477. He stayed in the Army after the war, rising to the rank of *Major* in October 1936, when he was appointed company commander with Infantry Regiment 103. At the start of the Second World War he was serving as Chief of Operations on the staff of the 13th Infantry Division with the rank of *Oberstleutnant*. From February 1940 he served as Chief of Operations on the Staff of XXXXI. Army Corps in the Netherlands and then Paris. From February 1941 he was Chief of the General Staff of the LVII. Army Corps and from June 1942 it was renamed the LVII. Panzer Corps. Fangohr also saw action in Russia.

Rudolf 'Rolf' LIPPERT

Generalmajor

* 29 October 1900, Leipzig
+ 1 April 1945, Schloss Neuhaus near Paderborn

Knight's Cross: Awarded on 9 June 1944 as *Oberst* and Commander of Panzer Regiment 31, part of the 5th Panzer Division, for actions in the Soviet Union. In April 1944 he was given the mission to attack and destroy Soviet forces that had penetrated the flank of the VI. Panzer Corps. For the mission he was given a battle group that consisted of two panzer regiments, an artillery regiment, an assault gun brigade and Hungarian Infantry Regiment 53. On 15 April his forces had captured Binduga in Poland and the following day another town had been taken, but his forces were fighting a well-organised partisan force. The terrain was difficult in and around Poland and Ukraine, where he took part in some bitter fighting against a strong Soviet force, and by the evening of 17 April a total of almost 400 Soviet soldiers had been killed, while the Germans had lost only forty-six dead and ninety-seven wounded. On 20 April Lippert's forces established contact with elements of the 214th Infantry Division near Zablocie, Poland, and fighting continued for the next few days. On 25 April his battle group was disbanded and the fighting was over. His forces had captured and destroyed most of the enemy forces, which included taking 466 prisoners, capturing twenty-six artillery guns, nineteen mortars, sixty-nine machine guns, 202 horse-drawn wagons, a large amount of ammunition and a field hospital. Lippert gave up his command in late July 1944 and entered the Reserves.

Rudolf Lippert entered the Army in June 1918 with Infantry Regiment 97 and later served with Rifle Regiment 49 and Rifle Regiment 8 before entering various courses. He was commissioned as a *Leutnant* in December 1922. In 1928 he took part in the Amsterdam Olympic Games, entering the equestrian three-day event, and was awarded a Gold Medal at the Berlin Olympic Games of 1936. From November 1938 he served as an instructor at the Army Riding and Transport School in Hannover, now with the rank of *Major*. In June 1940 he served as commander of Reconnaissance Battalion 9 and later served as commander of a bicycle training battalion, now with the rank of *Oberstleutnant*. He served as leader of the Panzer regiment Grossdeutschland and then attended the Tiger Panzer courses in Erlangen, now with the rank of *Oberst*. He later took over command of Panzer Regiment 31.

From 16 October he took over the leadership of the 5th Panzer Division. From November his command took part in the defensive battle of East Prussia and in January 1945 Lippert was promoted to *Generalmajor*. He saw brief action near Königsberg before becoming ill. He was evacuated out of the main area but was captured by US soldiers and seriously wounded, and as a result he died on 1 April 1945.

Gustav-Adolf von NOSTITZ-WALLWITZ

Generalmajor

* 11 July 1898, Oschatz, Saxony
+ 31 May 1945, Rögen near Eckernförde

Knight's Cross: Awarded on 12 June 1944 as *Oberst* and Commander of Panzer Artillery Regiment 89 while attached to the 24th Panzer Division for actions during the heavy fighting with Soviet troops in south Ukraine. Nostitz-Wallwitz attended a Panzer Officer Course and then the 11th Divisional Leaders' Course in Hirschberg from May 1944. From September he took over the leadership of the 2nd Panzer Division. At this time the division had been decimated during the Battle of Normandy in June and it took part in the unsuccessful counter-attack at Mortain in August. However, with only twenty-five tanks left, it was surrounded at Falaise. The following month it was sent back to Germany to be rebuilt and Nostitz-Wallwitz became the new Commander of the 24th Panzer Division, seeing action in the Ukraine area. In October his division was transferred to Hungary and took part in the counter-attack west of Debrecen, also taking heavy casualties during the unsuccessful defence of Kecskemét. On 9 November he was promoted to *Generalmajor* and saw more action against the

Gustav-Adolf von Nostitz-Wallwitz entered the Army with Field Artillery Regiment 12 in August 1917 and stayed in the service after the war. From October 1923 he served with Artillery Regiment 4 in Dresden and was promoted to *Hauptmann* in June 1933, when he attended the Cavalry School in Hannover. In October 1936 he was battalion commander with Artillery Regiment 22 and at the start of the Second World War he was serving as battalion commander with Artillery Regiment 216 with the rank of *Major*. He later served with the 1st Cavalry Division from late 1940 and was then assigned to the 24th Panzer Division in February 1942 with the rank of *Oberst*.

Soviets in Slovakia, Poland and East Prussia. In January 1945 the only combat units he had left were two tank companies, a panzer grenadier regiment and a single tank-destroyer battalion. Nostitz-Wallwitz was wounded near Pillau on 26 March but returned to his command after only a few days. The division was evacuated by sea to northern Germany in April 1945 and Nostitz-Wallwitz was appointed Commandant of Eckernförd. However, just a few days later he was seriously wounded and admitted to hospital, where he was taken prisoner by the Allies and on 31 May 1945 he died.

Hermann Heinrich Johann NIEHOFF

General der Infanterie

* 3 April 1897, Papenburg, Aschendorf
+ 5 November 1980, Riegsee

Knight's Cross: Awarded on 15 June 1944 as *Generalleutnant* and Commander of the 371st Infantry Division for his leadership and outstanding bravery on the Russian Front. Between 5 and 7 June 1944 his division defended its position by the Bug River and participated in the heavy fighting in northern Croatia and Ukraine. He continued to see action in this area during the latter stages of 1944 and in all this time his energy and drive was crucial in the fighting leadership of his division.

Knight's Cross with Oakleaves: He became the 764th recipient on 5 March 1945 as *Generalleutnant* and while still Commander of the 371st Infantry Division he was awarded the Oakleaves in recognition of his outstanding defence of Breslau in early 1945. In fact, the Soviet *Marshal* Zhukov said of Neihoff, 'a brave man. He is one of the few who I genuinely do admire. In my experience

Some records reported that Niehoff was awarded the Knight's Cross with Oakleaves and Swords on 26 April 1945 but no records were found in the Federal Archives to prove this. The Award Association of the Knight's Cross only assumed that Niehoff had received the Swords and that Niehoff himself had stated Gauleiter Hanke had recommended him for the award but there is no mention of this in Federal Archives. Photographs show Niehoff wearing the award of the Swords but it is thought that the photos were taken after the war when the Knight's Cross Association had presented him with them.

of the war General Niehoff has a place of honour.' During the subsequent battles against the Red Army in early 1945 in Upper Silesia, Niehoff continued to command his division with great skill and from March he took command of Fortress Breslau, which he held until the German surrender and he was promoted to *General der Infanterie* on 1 April 1945. The local *Gauleiter*, Karl Hanke, was against the surrender but Niehoff argued that its 140,000 civilians would need feeding and his troops consisted of a small 'rag-tag' force of *Luftwaffe*, Army and *Waffen-SS* troops. He was later sentenced to death by the Soviets for supposed war crimes but the sentence was commuted to twenty-five years' imprisonment. He was released on a general amnesty in October 1955 and returned to Germany.

Paul Otto Ferdinand BETZ

Generalmajor

* 10 July 1895, Harburg in Hamburg
+ 9 May 1944, Sevastopol, Soviet Union

Knight's Cross: Awarded posthumously on 16 June 1944 as *Oberst* and *Führer* of 50th Infantry Division, part of the XXXXIX. Mountain Corps, for his leadership and bravery during the fierce fighting near Sevastopol during the night of 8–9 May 1944. The Soviet forces had managed to cross the Severnaya Bay, and in response *Oberst* Betz led two battalions that broke through the enemy lines and recaptured the high ground near Nikolayevka. Betz was killed during an air raid on 9 May and was posthumously promoted to the rank of *Generalmajor* the following month.

Paul Betz entered the Army as a war volunteer in August 1914 and was commissioned as a *Leutnant* the following year while serving with Engineer Battalion 30. At the end of 1918, with war now over Betz left the Army and entered civilian life. In May 1934 he re-entered the Army and was attached to the Army Sports School in Wünsdorf, and from October 1937 he served as an instructor at the War School in Munich. He was serving on the staff of the Military Commander in Posen at the outbreak of war in September, saw action during the Polish campaign and from May 1941 he was attached to the Afrikakorps. In April 1944 he took over as fortress commander and from 2 May he was delegated with the leadership of the 50th Infantry Division and continued to see heavy action, once again around the area of Sevastopol.

Gerhard Michael ENGEL

Generalleutnant

* 13 April 1906, Guben, Brandenburg
+ 9 December 1976, Düsseldorf in North Rhine-Westphalia

Gerhard Engel entered Army service with the rank of *Gefreiter* in October 1925 and was attached to Infantry Regiment 5. He attended Infantry School from August 1927. He was commissioned as a *Leutnant* in September 1930 and was appointed company officer with his regiment and three years later he was promoted to *Oberleutnant*. From September 1933 he served as adjutant of the III. Battalion of his regiment and was appointed adjutant of Infantry Regiment 27 in October 1935. He was promoted to *Hauptmann* two years later.

Engel was appointed commander of the 11th Company of his regiment in October 1937 and from March 1938 until February 1944 he served as adjutant of the Wehrmacht to Adolf Hitler, now with the rank of *Oberstleutnant*.

Knight's Cross: Awarded on 4 July 1944 as *Oberstleutnant* and Commander of Füsilier Regiment 27 while attached to the 12th Infantry Division for his leadership and gallantry during the decisive battles near Minsk in the Soviet Union. He formed a battle group and was determined to break out. He then took virtual command of the division and formed another battle group, which fought through to Minsk and upon arriving they were once again encircled by Soviet forces. Engel was able to lead his men to safety but the bulk of the 12th Infantry Division was annihilated between 4 and 6 July 1944.

Knight's Cross with Oakleaves: He became the 679th recipient on 11 December 1944 as *Generalmajor* and Commander of 12th *Volksgrenadier* Division of the LXXXI. Army Corps for actions during the Ardennes Offensive. His command fought at the heart of the heavy combat during the second and third battles in Aachen and was always in the heart of the battle, acting as an inspiration to his men. The Oakleaves were personally presented to Engel by Hitler at Führer Headquarters Adlerhorst, Ziegenberg. In April 1945 Engel was promoted to the rank of *Generalleutnant* and took command of Infantry Division '*Ulrich von Hutten*', seeing action in the fighting in Berlin against the Red Army. He was captured by American forces on 8 May 1945 and remained in Allied captivity until December 1947.

Ernst MERK

Generalmajor

* 27 September 1903, Fürth
+ 12 June 1975, Munich

Knight's Cross: Awarded on 15 July 1944 as *Oberst im Generalstab* as Chief of the General Staff of the III. Panzer Corps for his leadership and bravery during the Soviet summer offensive around Galicia and Zolochiv in Ukraine. He briefly took over the leadership of the 16th Panzer Division from 6 to 14 August 1944 while *Generalmajor* Hans-Ulrich Back was away on leave. On 20 September he went into the Reserves to make ready for his transfer to become Chief of the General Staff of the 5th Panzer Army but this never happened as he was seriously wounded on 26 September and was hospitalised in Prague. In February 1945 Merk was appointed Deputy Leader of the Operations Department in the General Staff of the Army, and from early March he took over as Chief of the General Staff of the 18th Army under *General der Infanterie* Ehrenfried-Oskar Boege. Promoted to *Generalmajor* on 20 April 1945, he surrendered to Soviet forces in the Courland Pocket area on 11 May 1945 together with General Boege and both were sentenced to twenty-five years in a Labour Camp by a Soviet court in Moscow. Both were released in October 1955 and repatriated to Germany.

Friedrich-August WEINKNECHT

Generalleutnant

* 5 October 1895, Breslau
+ 26 October 1964, Gottingen

Knight's Cross: Awarded on 15 July 1944 as *Generalmajor* and Commander of the 79th Infantry Division while taking part in the retreat through Ukraine and into Romania, and for his leadership during the heavy fighting in the Nikopol

Bridgehead area in early 1944. He was described by a senior officer as having 'a lively personality, open, reliable character and brave in front of the enemy. Smart, tactically very good trained officer who led his division with great skill.' For his special commitment in the defensive fighting on both sides of Jassy he received the Knight's Cross and was promoted to the rank of *Generalleutnant*. In late August the Romanian army defected from the Axis, leaving the rebuilt 6th Army (not the army it had been) and much of Army Group South *Ukraine*, which included Weinknechts' 79th Infantry Division, cut off. The division tried to push its way through Soviet lines together with *General der Infanterie* Friedrich Mieth's IV. Army Corps, but was almost destroyed by the Red Army near the village of Chitcani on the Bârlad River. Mieth was later killed during the heavy fighting and Weinknecht and his men were taken prisoner on 29 August 1944 by Soviet soldiers and later sentenced to prison. However, he later joined the People's Armed Forces of East Germany and became an officer in the National Committee to Free Germany.

Konrad Georg Ludwig Edmund BLAUROCK

Generalleutnant

* 12 October 1899, Nuremberg
+ 25 January 1966, Nuremberg

Knight's Cross: Awarded on 27 July 1944 as *Oberst im Generalstab* and Commander of Grenadier Regiment 320, part of the 212th Infantry Division, in recognition of his bravery and leadership during the heavy fighting near Vitebsk on the Russian Front. On 1 October Blaurock was promoted to *Generalmajor* and took command of the 56th Infantry Division, seeing action in East Prussia as part of the XXVI. Army Corps.

Knight's Cross with Oakleaves: He became the 746th recipient on 19 February 1945 as *Generalmajor* and Commander of the 56th Infantry Division in recognition of his attempts to slow down the Soviet offensive, which gained time for the 4th Army so it was able to breakout. In January and February 1945 the Soviet offensive pushed the 3rd Panzer Army west towards Königsberg, where the division was finally encircled in the Heiligenbeil Pocket. Only about 250 men managed to break out alongside Blaurock and with the 18th Panzer Grenadier Division they headed westwards to Pomerania, where it was reformed into Infantry Division *Ulrich von Hutten** and Blaurock became its commander. He was promoted to *Generalleutnant* on 1 April and on the 19th took over as

Edmund Blaurock entered the Army in March 1918, and was sent to the Western Front. He was commissioned as a *Leutnant* during the final month of the war. After the war he joined the *Freikorps Epp*. From June 1938 he served as Chief of Operations of the 8th Infantry Division and saw action during the Polish campaign from September 1939 as part of the VIII. Army Corps. His division broke through strong enemy frontier fortifications in eastern Upper Silesia and later took part in the advance on Kracow. From May 1940 his division took part in the French campaign as part of the 4th Army and after the surrender remained in France on occupation duty. In March 1941 he was assigned to the 9th Army as Chief of Operations and saw action on the Eastern Front as part of Army Group B, later seeing action during the fierce fighting of the Soviet winter offensive as part of Army Group Centre. From July until October 1941 his division took part in the advance on Bialystok and Minsk and then on Moscow.

Commander of the 5th *Jäger* Division, which he led during some of the final battles around Berlin in which most of the division was destroyed. However, remnants along with Blaurock managed to escape and surrendered to British troops on 3 May 1945.

* *Ulrich von Hutten (21 April 1488–29 August 1523) was a German knight, poet and satirist, who later became a Protestant reformer, and who by 1519 was an outspoken critic of the Roman Catholic Church.*

Gustav Dietrich Adolf HEISTERMANN VON ZIEHLBERG

Generalleutnant

* 10 December 1898, Hohensalza
+ 2 February 1945, Berlin-Spandau

Knight's Cross: Awarded on 27 July 1944 as *Generalleutnant* and Commander of the 28th *Jäger* Division for actions near Lake Ladoga in the Soviet Union. Later his command was attached to Group *von Saucken* and took part in the effort to prevent the encirclement of the bulk of the 4th Army near Minsk, but failed. His command later suffered heavy losses in the retreat into Poland, where Heistermann von Ziehlberg led it during the heavy fighting near the old Brest-Litovsk fortress in Poland. On 19 November 1944 he was arrested in connection with the 20 July 1944 bomb plot to kill Hitler. Heistermann von Ziehlberg had been involved in the procurement of the explosives for the assassination

Gustav Heistermann von Ziehlberg joined the Army in August 1914 and served as a platoon leader. He was commissioned as a *Leutnant* in May 1915. He later served as weapons officer with Grenadier Regiment 2 and was at the same time temporary adjutant and ended the war as a company leader. He stayed in the Army after the war and from October 1935 he was served as company commander in Infantry Regiment 50 with the rank of *Hauptmann*. At the start of the Second World War he was attached to Army Group South with the rank of *Oberstleutnant* and from December he served as Head of the Central Department of the Army General Staff. In January 1941 he served as commander of Infantry Regiment 48 of the 12th Infantry Division and was promoted to *Oberst* in February. From May 1943 he took over as commander of the 65th Infantry Division and was promoted to *Generalmajor* in August 1943. In November he was severely wounded in battle, losing an arm.

attempt on Hitler. Sentenced to death by the Reich Supreme Military Court in Torgau, and with the loss of all military awards, he was executed by firing squad on 2 February 1945.

Max Ludwig Eduard Ferdinand LINDIG

Generalleutnant

* 11 July 1887, Berlin
+ 26 April 1961, Itzehoe

Max Lindig entered the Army as a volunteer in October 1909 and was commissioned as a *Leutnant* in March 1911. At the start of the First World War he served with Field Artillery Regiment 18, later serving as a battery leader and adjutant of Mobile Field Artillery Replacement Battalion 4. Promoted to *Hauptmann* in April 1918, he remained in the Army after the war and served with Artillery Regiment 2 until 1932. From October 1935 he served as Commander of I. Battalion of Artillery Regiment 56 with the rank of *Oberstleutnant* and the following year he transferred into the Reich War Ministry. Promoted to *Oberst* in January 1937, he was named as commander of Artillery Regiment 9 in June 1939 and from April 1940 he served as Artillery Commander 122, seeing action in the invasion of France. He was promoted to *Generalmajor* in December 1940 and from March 1942 was appointed Higher Artillery Commander 307 and saw action on the Eastern Front.

Knight's Cross: Awarded on 20 July 1944 as *Generalleutnant* and Higher Artillery Commander 307 for actions on the Eastern Front while attached to the 9th Army, and at the same time he was Battle Commandant of Asipovichy in Belarus. From August until the end of December he rested in the *Führer* Reserve and then served as Higher Artillery Commander of the Parachute Army. He surrendered to Western Allies in May 1945 and was held in captivity until his release in 1947.

Wilhelm Otto Oswald HASSE

General der Infanterie

* 24 November 1894, Schepankowitz, Bohemia
+ 6 June 1945, Eichhäusel, Silesia

Knight's Cross: Awarded on 12 August 1944 as *Generalleutnant* and Commander of the 30th Infantry Division while attached to the XXVIII. Army Corps for his outstanding leadership during actions in the summer of 1944 around Daugavpils in Latvia. Hasse had been temporary commander of the II. Army Corps from March 1944 and was presented his medal by the Commanding General of the 16th Army *General der Infanterie*, Paul Laux.

Knight's Cross with Oakleaves: He became the 698th recipient on 14 January 1945 as *General der Infanterie* and Commanding General of the II. Army Corps part of the 18th Army for his distinguished service during the Second Battle

Wilhelm Hasse entered the Army in October 1913 with Fusilier Regiment 86 and at the start of the First World War served as a platoon leader. He was promoted to *Leutnant* in October 1914. He was wounded three times between 1914 and 1916 and served as company leader, battalion adjutant and later as regimental adjutant. He was promoted to *Oberleutnant* in June 1918. Hasse remained in the Army after the war, rising to the rank of *Oberstleutnant* in August 1936, and from September 1938 he served as Chief of Operations in the General Staff of Group Command 1 in Berlin. Promoted to *Oberst* in March 1939, he served as Chief of Operations in the General Staff of Army Group North of Army Group B from September and saw action during the invasion of the Soviet Union the following year. From January 1942 he served as Chief of the General Staff of Army Group North and was promoted to *Generalmajor* in February 1942.

of Courland in Latvia from November 1944. He proved himself an excellent commander during the battles and there was a real concern that the Soviets could have split the 18th Army in half. However, his leadership and bravery contributed significantly in preventing such a defeat and he was recognised for his efforts with the award. He continued to see action in the Courland area until he was wounded on 8 May 1945 and that same day he was taken prisoner by Soviet troops, but wasn't given any medical attention. On 21 May he died while in the prison camp in Pisek, Czechoslovakia.

Heinrich KITTEL
Generalleutnant

* 31 October 1892, Gerolzhofen, Schweinfurt
\+ 5 March 1969, Bad Tolz

Knight's Cross: Awarded on 12 August 1944 as *Generalmajor* and Battle Commandant of Lviv in western Ukraine for actions during the fierce fighting against Soviet troops. Shortly after receiving his Knight's Cross he was promoted

Heinrich Kittel entered Army service as a *Fahnenjunker* with Bavarian Infantry Regiment 2 in July 1911 and he attended War School in Munich in 1914. Having been commissioned as a *Leutnant* the year before, he served as a platoon and company leader during the First World War. He remained in the Army after the war and from October 1936 served as battalion commander with Infantry Regiment 42 with the rank of *Oberstleutnant*. At the start of the Second World War he served as commander of Infantry Regiment 42 and was promoted to *Oberst* in April 1938. Between May 1942 and November 1944, during which time he was promoted to *Generalmajor*, he served as Commandant of Stalino, Rostov, Zaporozhye, Krivoy Rog, Uman and Lvov.

to *Generalleutnant* and appointed Commandant of Kracow in Poland. He stayed there until early November 1944, when Hitler ordered him to Metz to take over as Commandant. Kittel was sent there as an expert on fortress warfare and he told Hitler that the garrison would fight to the last man. Kittel decided that he would concentrate manpower and resources to hold four of Metz's strongest forts, all of which were located on the west bank. At this time he was also made the new commander of the 462nd *Volksgrenadier* Division, succeeding Vollrath Lübbe, who had suffered a stroke. However, on 17 November Kittel was seriously wounded and a few days later was captured while recovering in hospital. Only 1,100 of Kittel's men managed to escape the fall of fortress Metz, almost all of whom were wounded, and he remained in US captivity until his release in 1947.

Johann Karl Friedrich PFLUGBEIL

Generalleutnant

* 24 August 1882, Hütten, Pima
\+ 21 October 1951, Stuttgart

Knight's Cross: Awarded on 12 August 1944 as *Generalleutnant* and Commander of Field Training Division North and Battle Commander *Mitau* for his actions in the simultaneous function as a fighter commander of Jelgava in Latvia. In early February 1945 Pflugbeil was appointed commander of Infantry Division Kurland and he returned to the Baltic area shortly before the end of the war. It

Johann Pflugbeil is seen here with his brother General Curt Pfugbeil of the *Luftwaffe*. Johann took command of the 221st Security Division on 27th June 1941 and took control of the Polish city of Bialystok, which had been in the Soviet zone of occupation. On that same day a police battalion had begun to arrest, beat and shoot members of the local Jewish community and their chiefs went to see Pflugbeil and begged him to stop the pogrom, but he ignored them. The pogrom became a slaughter and 700 Jews were killed and their corpses piled high and burned. In March 1942 he took command of a large-scale security operation against so-called partisans and ordered his troops to kill all 'partisans'. His unit shot 806 enemies of the state and another 120 were handed over to the Secret Field Police for execution. He was never charged with war crimes.

was there he was captured by the British and remained in captivity until 1947. He was the older brother of *General der Flieger* Kurt Pflugbeil, winner of the Knight's Cross with Oakleaves.

Otto Werner Friedrich Constantin Baron DIGEON VON MONTEON

Generalmajor

* 28 February 1886, Bernburg, Saale
+ 27 June 1944, near Gorodez, South-west Lepel, Soviet Union

Constantin Digeon von Monteon entered the Army in March 1905 as a *Leutnant* with Queen Elisabeth Guards Grenadier Regiment 3. At the start of the First World War he was serving as a machine-gun leader with Machine-Gun Battalion 6 and later as a *Hauptmann* he served as a General Staff Officer. He retired from the Army in 1920 but returned with the rank of *Major* in October 1933 as a Territorial officer and later served as training director at Bartensetin, Hesse.

Knight's Cross: Awarded posthumously on 14 August 1944 as *Oberst* and Commander of the Army Weapons School with Panzer Army Headquarters 3 and Battle Commandant of Fortress *Lepel* for actions in Vitebsk. Digeon von Monteon was at the time taking part in Operation Bagration, the code name for the 1944 Soviet Byelorussian strategic offensive operation between 22 June and 19 August 1944. On 27 June the Soviets attacked the German lines and many of the enemy penetrations of the front were defeated by Digeon von Monteon's battle groups. It was during these attacks that he was killed.

He was promoted to *Oberstleutnant* in October 1938 he was appointed commander of Infantry Regiment 311 from August 1939 while attached to the 217th Infantry Division. He saw action during the Polish campaign and later in northern France and on the Eastern Front, where he was promoted to *Oberst* in October 1941.

Franz Heinrich Otto SENSFUSS

Generalleutnant

* 21 June 1891, Trunz, Elbing
+ 11 March 1976, Heppenheim

Knight's Cross: Awarded on 22 August 1944 as *Generalleutnant* and Commander of the 212th Infantry Division for his success in repelling numerous Soviet attacks north-west of Lake Narach in Belarus in mid-1944, during the retreat from the Baltic and Eastern Front. His division, however, later suffered during heavy defensive actions and was almost destroyed. In fact, the High Command of the Army disbanded the division and reformed it in September 1944 as the 212th *Volksgrenadier* Division.

Knight's Cross with Oakleaves: Sensfuss became the 881st recipient on 9 May 1945 as *Generalleutnant* and while still commanding the 212th *Volksgrenadier* Division for his skill and leadership in helping to secure an important hilltop position during a tank battle in 9 August 1944. He also fought hard during the fighting at Weilerbach, Germany, and Echternach in Luxembourg, as part of the 7th Army during the Battle of the Bulge. The award was supported by *SS-Reichsführer* Heinrich Himmler and by *Generalfeldmarschall* Walter Model. However, the award recommendation arrived from the battlefield at the Army Personnel Office on 14 March 1945 and was put on hold when it was reported that Sensfuss had been captured and reported as missing. The award was never approved, and the award number came from the Award Association of the

Franz Sensfuss joined the Army as a volunteer in October 1910 with Baden Field Artillery Regiment No. 76 in Freiburg and studied law. He served in the First World War and was awarded the Iron Cross 1st and 2nd Classes. By the end of the war he had been promoted to *Oberleutnant*. He stayed in the Army after the war, rising to the rank of *Major* in February 1934, when he was serving on the Staff of the 3rd Cavalry Brigade in Hannover. From November 1938 he served as commander of Cavalry Regiment 3 and in December 1939 he was appointed commander of Mounted Regiment 22, now with the rank of *Oberst*. He saw action in the French campaign and from July 1940 he was head of the German delegation to the Italian–French Armistice Commission. Promoted to *Generalmajor* in 1941, he later served as commander of the 17th Panzer Division and was promoted to *Generalleutnant* in May 1943.

Knight's Cross and is therefore illegal. Sensfuss had in fact not been captured at the time but he did surrender to US forces on 10 May 1945 and was released in 1947.

Rolf Fritz Karl Willy WUTHMANN

General der Artillerie

* 26 August 1893, Kassel
\+ 20 October 1977, Minden

Knight's Cross: Awarded on 22 August 1944 as *General der Artillerie* and Commanding General of the IX. Army Corps, part of the 3rd Panzer Army, for actions in the Soviet Union. He took part in the retreat via Plisa and Kazyany in Belarus and reached Ukmerge in Lithuania in late July 1944. He received a positive assessment from *Generaloberst* Georg-Hans Reinhardt, the commander of the 3rd Panzer Army, who said, 'Wuthmann is fresh, energetic and has an enthusiastic manner and is tactically well educated.' In fact, at the beginning of the Soviet summer offensive his corps had been badly hit but escaped encirclement, and in October the Red Army had made a breakthrough and his command was once again in retreat. Since mid-December the Jüra River near Taurage in Lithuania had frozen over and no longer formed a natural obstacle. Then in mid-January 1945 the Soviets opened the Battle of East Prussia and by 20 January German resistance was lost; the 69th and 56th Infantry Divisions

Rolf Wuthmann entered the Army in April 1912 and was commissioned as a *Leutnant* in November 1913, seeing action with Reserve Artillery Regiment 6. He was appointed battalion adjutant and later a battery commander. He was awarded both classes of the Iron Cross, staying in the Army after the war. Promoted to *Major* in August 1934, he was later attached to the Transport Department of the Army General Staff and from November 1938 he was Chief of Operations on the Staff of Army Group Command 6. In August 1939 he was appointed Chief of Operations of the 4th Army and from November 1940 he served in a similar capacity with the 16th Army. He was promoted to *Generalmajor* in February 1942. In April he was appointed Chief of the General Staff of the 15th Army and from May he was commander of the 295th Infantry Division. From June 1943 he was commander of the 112th Infantry Division and had by now been promoted to the rank of *Generalleutnant*.

were in retreat towards Königsberg. On 20 April Wuthmann was ordered to defend the island of Bornholm in Denmark and from that day he basically gave up his command of his army corps. The Soviets attacked the island, the only part of Denmark they actually invaded, and he was captured and remained in Soviet captivity until his release on 9 November 1955.

Hermann Otto Eduard FOERTSCH

General der Infanterie

* 4 April 1885, Drahnow, Deutsch-Krone
+ 27 December 1961, Munich

Knight's Cross: Awarded on 27 August 1944 as *Generalleutnant* and Commander of the 21st Infantry Division for his leadership in the summer of 1944 in response to a Soviet breakthrough when he launched a successful counter-attack and closed a front-line gap east of Lake Hino in Estonia. On 9 November 1944 Foertsch was promoted to *General der Infanterie* and appointed Commanding General of the X. Army Corps, seeing action in Latvia as part of Army Group North. After a period in the Reserves, he was given the temporary leadership of the 19th Army on the Western Front. On 3 March 1945 he took command of the 1st Army and saw action against Allied troops in the area of the Rhine. His command was encircled near the town of Kaiserslautern in south-west Germany, where he surrendered to US troops. He was released from captivity in February 1948 after being acquitted at the Nuremberg Trials as part of Case Number 7.

Hermann Foertsch entered Army service with Infantry Regiment 175 in March 1913 and was commissioned as a *Leutnant* the following year. He stayed with the Army after the war with Infantry Regiment 17 before being transferred to the Troop Office as an adjutant in October 1924. He later served as company commander and in August 1932 he served as press chief and leader of the Inland Department with the Reich War Ministry and was promoted to *Oberstleutnant* in January 1936. He later transferred into the Army General Staff and was tactics instructor at the War Academy from February 1937, and from August 1939 he was Chief of the General Staff of the Replacement VIII. Army Corps. Two months later he took over as Chief of the General Staff of XXVI. Army Corps. In February 1942 he was promoted to *Generalmajor* and in January 1943 was appointed Chief of the General Staff of Army Group E.

Ernst Wilhelm Albert KNEBEL

Generalmajor

* 2nd June 1892, Naunhof, Grimma
+ 13 March 1945, Prussian Eylau (hospital)

Knight's Cross: Awarded on 27 August 1944 as *Oberst* and Commander of Field Replacement Regiment with Headquarters of Panzer Army 3 for actions during the heavy fighting on the border of East Prussia in the summer of 1944. In September he left front-line duty and became commander of the Army Weapons School of the 3rd Panzer Army.

Knight's Cross with Oakleaves: Awarded on 19 February 1945 to become the 745th recipient as *Oberst* and Commander of Army Training Centre School of the Headquarters of Panzer Army 3 for his actions in January 1945. From mid-January until his death in March, Knebel commanded an ad hoc unit comprised of *Volkssturm* members (older men and young boys of the Hitler Youth), and although outnumbered by the enemy these units managed to hold the German front between the Curonian Lagoon of the Baltic Sea in Lithuania to the Masurian Lakes in Poland. He was promoted to *Generalmajor* on 1 March and during these battles Knebel was seriously wounded and taken to hospital, where he died. He has no known grave.

Ernst Knebel entered the Army as a war volunteer in April 1914 with Dragoon Regiment 11 and was commissioned as a *Leutnant* the following year. He later served as a company officer with Infantry Regiment 104 and then as an adjutant with the rank of *Oberleutnant*. He left the Army after the war and joined the police, rising to the rank of *Polizei-Major* in April 1933, before returning to the Army in 1935. He served for a time as an Army instructor and from November 1940 served as commander of Infantry Regiment 580, now with the rank of *Oberst*. He was wounded and hospitalised from August 1943, returning to combat as commander of Jäger Regiment 268 from January 1944.

Werner Wolfgang SCHMIDT-HAMMER

Generalleutnant

* 26 September 1894, Hartmannsdorf, Rochlitz
+ 4 January 1962, Landau

Knight's Cross: Awarded on 2 September 1944 as *Generalleutnant* and Commander of the 168th Infantry Division, part of the 1st Panzer Army, for his leadership during the heavy fighting in the Tarnopol and the Carpathian Mountain area. He later led his division during the battles on the Vistula in early 1945, including the Baranow Bridgehead, on the Vistula, where it was smashed. In April he was appointed the successor to the *General der Infanterie* Anton Grasser as leader of the LXXII. Army Corps while still attached to the 1st Panzer Army. In May he surrendered to the Soviets in Czechoslovakia and he was deported to the Soviet Union, spending just over ten years in prison camps. On 7 January 1956 he was finally released, one of the last generals to be returned to Germany, together with *Generaloberst* Rudolf Schmidt, *General der Infanterie* Kurt Röpke, *Generalleutnant* Hermann Boettcher and five other senior commanders.

Paul Rudolf SCHÜRMANN

Generalmajor

* 6 December 1895, Eiringhausen Gmde, Plettenberg
+ 1 February 1978, Wiesbaden

Knight's Cross: Awarded on 2 September 1944 as *Generalmajor* and Commander of the 25th Panzer Grenadier Division for actions during the fierce fighting in Orsha in Belarus on the Eastern Front. Shortly after being presented with the award he became seriously ill. He had contracted an illness during a forty-six-day march from the Minsk Pocket area. He never returned to duty, in fact his medical certificate estimated that he would not be fit for duty until after 1 July 1945. His command of his division was handed over to *Generalmajor* Arnold Burmeister.

Clemens BETZEL

Generalleutnant

* 9 June 1895, Ulm an der Donau, Württemberg
+ 27 March 1945, near Gdansk, Poland

Clemens Betzel remained in the Army after the war, serving in the *Reichswehr* 21st Artillery Regiment, and then with the 7th Artillery Regiment. He was promoted to *Hauptmann* in May 1928. He retired from the Army in September 1930, deciding to study economics at the technical college in Munich, but he left after just one term. From April 1931 he was employed as a Landwehr officer (National Defence), attached to Military District Command VII in Munich, and from October 1933 was a member of the SA.

Knight's Cross: Awarded on 5 September 1944 as *Generalmajor* and Commander of the 4th Panzer Division, part of the XXXIX. Army Corps, in recognition of his bravery and leadership on the Eastern Front. On 3 July 1944 Betzel, with his division, launched swift attacks towards the north via Nieswiez, and succeeded in capturing two other towns. This enabled the 12th Panzer Division to capture the southern bank of the river near Stowbtsy in Belarus.

Knight's Cross with Oakleaves: He became the 774th recipient on 11 March 1945 as *Generalleutnant* and Commander of the 4th Panzer Division while

In June 1941 he took part in the invasion of the Soviet Union, where his battalion was involved in the bitter fighting at Minsk, Gomel, Kiev, Bryansk and Vyazma on the road to Moscow, and by November the 4th Panzer Division only had fifty operational tanks left. Betzel was appointed commander of Artillery Regiment 103 on 20 November and by December his troops had attempted to encircle the city of Tula, south-east of Moscow. However, this failed and again the entire division suffered heavy losses during the attempt. Betzel was awarded the German Cross in Gold on 11 March 1943 while an *Oberst* commanding Panzer Artillery Regiment 103 for his part in the success artillery attacks near Novhorod-Siverskyi.

attached to the XXXXVI. Army Corps in recognition for his part in the success in preventing the breakthrough by Soviet forces in West Prussia. In just five days the 4th Panzer Division had destroyed 113 tanks and forty-one heavy anti-tank guns. From January until March his division was deployed in the areas around Schwetz-Tuchele Moor, Bütow and Karthaus, in West Prussia and Germany. During heavy fighting near Gdansk, at about 1600 hrs Betzel was hit by an enemy bullet and killed. He is buried today at the Danzig Garrison Cemetery and lies in Plot 1A, Row 1, Grave No. 9.

Friedrich Albert FOERTSCH

Generalleutnant

* 19 May 1900, Drahnow, West Prussia
+ 14 December 1976, Goslar, Lower Saxony

Knight's Cross: Awarded on 5 September 1944 as *Generalmajor* and Chief of the General Staff of the 18th Army for his leadership during the successful and decisive battles in the Soviet Union. He was presented with the award by the Commander-in-Chief of Army Group North *Generaloberst* Ferdinand Schörner on 7 September 1944. Foertsch was praised for his leadership and success during the defensive actions near Leningrad, at Volkhov and south of Lake Ladoga and in the defensive fighting in the Baltic region. From 25 January 1945 he was Chief of the General Staff of Army Group Courland under *Generaloberst* Carl Hilpert. Foertsch saw action in the Courland area and was promoted to *Generalleutnant* in March 1945. He surrendered to the Red Army in May 1945 and was imprisoned until 9 October 1955, joining the *Bundeswehr* a year later.

Friedrich Foertsch entered Army service with Infantry Regiment 175 in May 1918 and was commissioned with the rank of *Leutnant* in April 1922. From April 1935 he was attached to the staff of the Command Office in Königsberg and was promoted to *Major* in August 1938. He served as company commander with Infantry Regiment 81 and from October 1939 he served as Chief of Operations on the General Staff of the 60th Infantry Division. From July 1940 he was appointed Group Leader I on the Staff of the Chief of Army Armaments and commander of the Replacement Army *Generaloberst* Friedrich Fromm. Foertsch was promoted to *Oberst* in July 1942 and appointed Chief of Operations on the General Staff of the 18th Army. He was the brother of *General der Infanterie* Hermann Foertsch.

Werner Hans Willi NEUMANN

Generalmajor

* 13 May 1905, Neu-Beelitz, Bromberg
+ 4 July 1970, Lübeck

Knight's Cross: Awarded on 5 September 1944 as *Oberst* and Commander of Grenadier Regiment 121 while attached to the 50th Infantry Division for actions in the Soviet Union, where the German division suffered heavy losses. Neumann later led his regiment across East Prussia and towards the Böhr River in Czechoslovakia. After a ten-day rest in the Reserves, he attended the 16th Divisional Leaders' Course in Hirschberg from 21 November. Towards the end of February 1945 Neumann was given the leadership of the 563rd *Volksgrenadier* Division, succeeding *Generalmajor* Ferdinand Brühl. By the time Neumann took over the division was already down to battle group strength and had suffered huge losses in the Courland Pocket. Neumann was promoted to *Generalmajor* on 20 April 1945 and continued to command his division in the Courland area, where he surrendered to Red Army troops on 8 May 1945. He was imprisoned by the Soviets and was not returned to his homeland until 7 October 1955.

Erich Paul SEIDEL

Generalmajor

* 10 March 1900, Berlin
+ 11 April 1945, Straubenhardt-Conweiler in Baden-Württemberg

Knight's Cross: Awarded on 10 September 1944 as *Oberst* and Commander of Grenadier Regiment 236 while attached to the 69th Infantry Division for actions on the Eastern Front. Seidel first saw action during the fighting in Volkhov in early 1943, and later took part in the fighting on the northern sector near Leningrad. His regiment was later involved in the retreats on the northern sector of the front as part of Army Group Centre. Towards the end of October 1944 he attended the 15th Divisional Commanders' Course and from early November he took command of the 257th *Volksgrenadier* Division, which had been formed from the 257th Infantry Division. At the beginning of 1945 he saw action in the Alsace and in the Saar region, fighting at Zweibrücken, and he was promoted to *Generalmajor* on 8 February 1945. He later took part in the unsuccessful defence of Karlsruhe on the Rhine River and he was killed in action near Straubenhardt-Conweiler in Germany in April 1945.

Christian Leopold Ernst USINGER

Generalleutnant

* 21 August 1894, Wilhelmshaven
+ 2 April 1949 Camp Šuja, Ivanovo, Soviet Union

Christian Usinger joined the Army as a volunteer in August 1914 and was assigned to the East Prussian Foot Artillery Regiment for the duration of the First World War. He joined the police after the war and served in Berlin, rising to the rank of *Polizei-Major* just before he left in 1935 to rejoin the army. From October he was assigned to Artillery Regiment 13 and was promoted to *Oberst* in October 1940. From December 1941 he served as Artillery Commander 146. He was appointed temporary commander of the 223rd Infantry Division and his command became permanent when he was promoted to *Generalmajor* in December 1942.

Knight's Cross: Awarded on 15 September 1944 as *Generalmajor* and as Deputy Leader of the 81st Infantry Division for his leadership during the retreat through the Baltic States. Since October 1943 he had been appointed Higher Artillery Commander 315 and had been promoted to the rank of *Generalleutnant*. From 17 March 1945 he briefly led the XXXVIII. Panzer Corps while *General der Artillerie* Kurt Herzog was on leave and on 20 April he took command of the I. Army Corps in the Courland Pocket as part of the 18th Army. He surrendered to Soviet troops on 8 May 1945 and was imprisoned in various prison camps, which included Nr. 27, Krasnogorsk, Nr: 48 Černcy, Ležnevo and Nr. 3840 Šuja. He died from pulmonary tuberculosis while in captivity on 2 April 1949 and is buried in Šuja, Ivanovo Cemetery, Square 3, Grave No. 3.

Joseph Maria Hermann Ernst Peter Hans von RADOWITZ

Generalleutnant

* 29 July 1899, Frankfurt am Main
+ 1 June 1956, Bad Wiessee

Knight's Cross: Awarded on 17 September 1944 as *Oberst* and leader of the 23rd Panzer Division for his outstanding leadership during fighting on the Eastern Front. Between 29 July and 1 August 1944 Radowitz led his division in battle near Sandomierz in Poland and the following week he took part in offensive

Joseph von Radowitz entered the Army in June 1917 and was commissioned as a *Leutnant* the following year. He saw action with Dragoon Regiment 20 and remained in the Army after the war, rising to the rank of *Hauptmann* in February 1934. In October 1935 he was company commander with the 1st Mounted Regiment and from 1938 he served as adjutant on the Staff of the III. Army Corps in Berlin with the rank of *Major*. At the start of the Second World War he served as commander of Battalion 168 in Fürstenwalde, Germany, and later served as adjutant with the III. Army Corps. He was promoted to *Oberstleutnant* in 1941 and was appointed adjutant of the 2nd Panzer Army. In May 1943 he attended a regimental leaders' course at the Panzer School and from July he took over as leader of Panzer Grenadier Regiment 28, now with the rank of *Oberst*.

and defensive fighting near the city of Mielec, also in Poland. Towards the end of 1944 his division transferred to Hungary and took part in the counter-attack on Nyiregyhaza. In late October he took the town, destroying 600 Soviet tanks. He later led his division during the counter-attack west of Debrecen, and Radowitz was once again cited for distinguished conduct.

Knight's Cross with Oakleaves: Awarded on 9 May 1945 to become the 882nd recipient as *Generalleutnant* and Commander of the 23rd Panzer Division for continued actions on the Eastern Front. During ten days of bitter fighting under his command, his division repeatedly succeeded in bringing far superior enemy forces to a halt and thereby prevented a breakthrough. Radowitz was a brave and talented commander and during the very heavy fighting some other formations fled the field without their leaders. However Radowitz, a highly respected commander, never let go of his unit's reins. On 1 March 1945 he was promoted to *Generalleutnant* and early the following month his division was assigned the task of striking into the deep southern flank of enemy forces advancing westwards. Later Radowitz's leadership was the primary factor that thwarted Soviet forces from eliminating eight German divisions on the northern side of the Mura River. The last friendly forces were able to evacuate the bridgehead under the protection of the 23rd Panzer Division. In late April Radowitz was recommended for the Oakleaves and the award was endorsed by *General der Artillerie* Maximilian de Angelis. The award recommendation document arrived at the Army Personnel Office on 30 April 1945 but the recommendation was insufficient. On 2 May a teletype message was sent to the headquarters of the 2nd Panzer Army to be approved, but the award was disapproved, stating that the guidelines for approval of such an award had not been fulfilled. On 10 May 1945 Radowitz was captured by British forces near Steiermark and was subsequently released two years later. However in post-war years the Knight's Cross Association looked into Radowitz's award of the Oakleaves and decided to present him with the award, making him the unofficial 882nd recipient.

Gustav HARTENECK

General der Kavallerie

* 27 July 1892, Landau
+ 7 February 1984, Grosshesslohe, Munich

Knight's Cross: Awarded on 21 September 1944 as *General der Kavallerie* and Commanding General of the I. Cavalry Corps for actions between July and August 1944 during the German retreat via Bialystok towards Łomża in Poland. Harteneck was presented personally the Knight's Cross by the Commander-in-Chief of Army Group Centre, *Generaloberst* Georg-Hans Reinhardt, on 23 September 1944. At the beginning of October his corps saw action against Soviet troops in the town of Ostrołęka in Poland and later that month moved further north towards Augustów. By December his command had moved to Hungary, where it took part in the relief of the besieged capital Budapest and

Gustav Harteneck entered Army service as a war volunteer with Bavarian Regiment 3 in August 1914 and was commissioned as a *Leutnant* in August 1915. The following year he was awarded the Iron Cross 2nd Class and now saw action as part of the Bavarian Chevauleger Regiment 5 and attended various officer courses and a machine gun course. When the war ended he transferred into the *Freikorps* and was promoted to *Oberleutnant* in May 1923. He attended more courses and had been promoted to the rank of *Major* by August 1934. From October 1935 he served as Chief of Operations on the General Staff of the III. Army Corps, and at the start of the Second World War he served as Chief of Operations in the General Staff of the 1st Army with the rank of *Oberst* and saw action in France. He then served as Chief of the General Staff of the XXVII. Army Corps from November 1940 and almost a year later he was appointed Chief of the General Staff of the 2nd Army, seeing action on the Eastern Front. By April 1943 he held the rank of *Generalleutnant* while commander of the 72nd Infantry Division.

later during the fighting near Lake Balaton. The Soviet counteroffensive began on 16 March 1945 and the German troops were pushed back to their starting positions within a few days. By the end of March Harteneck had withdrawn his command back along the northern shore of Lake Balaton. On 26 April his corps withdrew to the area south-east of Graz during the fighting in south-east Styria, and they surrendered to the Western Allies on 8 May 1945.

Franz Max SCHLIEPER

Generalmajor

* 22 August 1905, Berlin-Friedenau
+ 4 April 1974, Munich

Knight's Cross: Awarded on 21 September 1944 as *Oberst im Generalstab* and Commander of Grenadier Brigade 1132 while attached to the 73rd Infantry Division for actions on the northern sector of the Eastern Front, seeing heavy action in Prague and Warsaw. In August he took command of the 73rd Infantry Division and continued to see action in the central sector of the Eastern Front. In December he was promoted to the rank of *Generalmajor*. In January 1945 his command faced a strong Soviet force with tanks and suffered serious losses, withdrawing along the Vistula front. Soon after the Soviets attacked again and the German division finally collapsed and was largely destroyed. Only a few staff members, including Schlieper, managed to escape from the Soviets.

Franz Schlieper entered the Army with Württemberg Infantry Regiment 13 in October 1925 and was commissioned as a *Leutnant* in December 1928. He served as a company officer with the 4th Prussian Infantry Regiment from 1929 and in October 1935 he served with Infantry Regiment 27 in Rostock with the rank of *Oberleutnant*. He was attached to the General Staff of Army Department 2 from October 1938 and at the start of the Second World War he was serving as a General Staff Officer with the 7th Army. He later served as Chief of Operations with Infantry Division 253 before being chief intelligence officer on the General Staff of the 9th Army from September 1941. Promoted to *Oberstleutnant* in April 1942, he was named Commander of Infantry Regiment 94 that same year and was promoted to *Oberst* in February 1943.

While still in the Danzig area, Schlieper took over the command of the 12th *Luftwaffe* Field Division on 10 April but within four weeks he had surrendered his command to Soviet forces. He was imprisoned in Camp No. 27 and then moved to Krasnogorsk Camp near Moscow. In June 1950 he was sentenced to twenty-five years' imprisonment in a labour camp by a Moscow Military Tribunal. He was released after a general amnesty was granted on 7 October 1955 and returned to Germany.

Paul Moritz REICHELT

Generalleutnant

* 29 March 1898, Neusalza, Löbau, Saxony
+ 22 September 1981, Munich, Bavaria

Knight's Cross: Awarded on 8 October 1944 as *Generalmajor* and Chief of the General Staff of Army Detachment *Narwa* for his leadership and duty as a staff officer while seeing action on the Eastern Front. In November he was transferred and became Chief of the General Staff of the 25th Army under the command of *Luftwaffe General der Flieger* Friedrich Christiansen while seeing action in the Netherlands. From 7 April his command became known as Fortress Holland and on the 20th Reichelt was promoted to *Generalleutnant* and his new commander was *Generaloberst* Johannes Blaskowitz. He continued to see heavy action in the Netherlands against British and American troops. On 7 May he surrendered to the British and was held in captivity until July 1947, when he returned to Germany.

Paul Reichelt entered the Army in September 1915 and saw action from April 1916 throughout the war with the 23rd Infantry Division. He stayed in the Army after the war and was commissioned as a *Leutnant* in December 1923 while serving with Infantry Regiment 11 for the next ten years. From October 1934 he attended the War Academy in Berlin and the following year was assigned to the War Ministry in Berlin. From October 1938 he served as Chief of Operations of the 7th Division in Munich, later seeing action in Poland, France and Belgium. In December 1941 he was Chief of the General Staff of the IX. Army Corps, seeing action on the Russian Front. From August 1943 served in a similar position with the XII. Army Corps and in January 1944, now with the rank of *Oberst*, he became deputy leader of the 299th Infantry Division while still assigned to the Eastern Front.

Johannes HÖLZ

Generalmajor

* 2 July 1906, Tigerfeld, Württemberg
+ 29 April 1945, Beelitz an der Elbe, Brandenburg

Knight's Cross: Awarded on 10 October 1944 as *Oberst im Generalstab* and Chief of the General Staff of the LV. Army Corps for his leadership during the heavy fighting near Bialystok and near the city of Łomża, north-east of Warsaw, in Poland in August–September 1944. A new front was formed on the northern bank of the Narew River and from November he witnessed heavy action near the Biebrza River, both in north-eastern Poland. On 30 November he was appointed Chief of the General Staff of the 9th Army and from early 1945 he saw action during the heavy fighting on the Vistula River in the Warsaw area. On 25 March Hölz was promoted to *Generalmajor* and on 18 April the Red Army broke through the German front and was able to carry out a pincer movement that led to the encirclement of the entire 9th Army. On 25 April, Hölz was ordered to attack westwards south of Berlin and unite with the 12th Army in order to liberate Berlin, but these orders were impossible to carry out. Hölz and his command had attempted to break out several times as part of the Battle of Halbe but had failed. On 29 April Hölz was killed the fierce fighting against Soviet troops near Beelitz an der Elbe in Brandenburg.

Johannes Hölz entered the police in May 1924, rising to the rank of *Polizei-Leutnant* in October 1930 when he transferred to Ellwangen Police headquarters. In April 1936 he transferred into the Army and was attached to Infantry Regiment 56 with the rank of *Oberleutnant*. From August 1939 he served on the General Staff and was attached to Army Group South. From the beginning of the Second World War he was on the staff of the Military Commander in Posen. In November he was appointed Chief Supply Officer on the Staff of the 14th Infantry Division and in March 1941 he was promoted to *Major*. Hölz was appointed Chief of Operations on the Staff of the 161st Infantry Division in July 1941 and from March 1942 he served as Chief of Operations on the General Staff of the 9th Army. He was promoted to *Oberst* in December 1943.

Horst Alexander Alfred Paul von MELLENTHIN

General der Artillerie

* 31 July 1898, Hannover
+ 8 January 1977, Wiesbaden

Knight's Cross: Awarded on 10 October 1944 as *Generalleutnant* and Commander of the 205th Infantry Division for actions during the heavy fighting in the Baltic region. His command prevented the Soviet breakthrough at Bauske in Latvia and the advance towards Riga and Polatsk in Belarus, distinguishing him as an excellent divisional commander. His command had successfully repulsed several attacks from superior forces, with his efforts and bravery being rewarded as in July he was promoted to the rank of *Generalleutnant*.

Knight's Cross with Oakleaves: He became the 815th recipient on 4 April 1945 as *Generalleutnant* and Commander of the 205th Infantry Division for his leadership and success in preventing an enemy breakthrough south-east of Frauenburg in Latvia during early March 1945. He was at this time serving as acting commander of the XXXVIII. Panzer Corps and during a ten-day period his troops destroyed more than 150 enemy tanks and forty-nine guns. He had taken command of the XXXVIII. Panzer Corps in January 1945 and from

Horst von Mellenthin entered the Army in January 1915 and was commissioned as a *Leutnant* six months later. He went onto serve as an ordnance officer on the Staff of the VI. Army Corps. From December 1916 he served as a battalion adjutant and from October 1918 he was a regimental adjutant. He stayed with the Army after the war, serving in various staff positions. By April 1936 had been promoted to the rank of *Major* and was serving as a battalion commander with the 1st Cavalry Brigade. In November 1938 he was leader of a General Staff Group in the Army and was promoted to *Oberstleutnant* in August 1939. The following year he served as Chief of the Military Attaché Branch on the General Staff of the Army. From December 1940 he served again as Chief of the Military Attaché Branch on the General Staff of the Army and in May 1943 he took command of Grenadier Regiment 67. In November he was commander of the 205th Infantry Division, and the following month he was promoted to *Generalmajor*. From 18 January until 21 February 1944 he took over as leader of the 23rd Infantry Division and then returned as commander of the 205th Infantry Division.

14 March he was named Commanding General of the XI. Army Corps. He showed great leadership when his troops pushed back Soviet forces who were attempting to break through the German lines, and for this he was promoted to *General der Artillerie.* On 20 April he was named Commanding General of the VIII. Army Corps in Upper Silesia and during the last days of the war saw action in Czechoslovakia, where he surrendered his command to American troops on 8 May 1945.

Joachim Ernst Oskar MUNZEL

Generalmajor

* 13 March 1899, Grimmen
+ 1 January 1992, Bad Godesberg

Knight's Cross: Awarded on 16 October 1944 as *Oberst* and temporary Commander of the 14th Panzer Division for actions in the northern sector of the Eastern Front and during the fighting in the Courland Pocket. During this time Munzel and his division played a major role in saving the 16th and 18th Armies, while opposing all six major Soviet attempts to isolate Army Group North. In December he was promoted to *Generalmajor* and from 15 January 1945 he was leader of Corps Group *Munzel*, an ad hoc battle unit, and from April he was Commander of the 2nd Panzer Division. He saw action against US troops and was by now down to the strength of just four tanks, three assault guns, and 200 men, fighting near Mosel along the Rhine and at Karlsbad-Pilsen. From 6 April he was appointed Higher Panzer Officer attached to the Commander-in-Chief West, *Generalfeldmarschall* Albert Kesselring, and ended the war in this post. He was kept in Allied captivity until May 1947 and was later that year employed by the Heinemann Company. From June 1951 he was a military advisor in Egypt. In May 1956 he joined the *Bundeswehr* and was appointed Commander of the Panzer School in Münster and later Inspector of Panzer Troops in Cologne until March 1962.

Gerha August Wolfgang Sophus POEL

Generalleutnant

* 7 February 1886, Wulmenau, Schleswig-Holstein
+ 8 August 1947, Krasnogorsk Prison Camp, Soviet Union

Knight's Cross: Awarded on 16 October 1944 as *Generalmajor* and Commandant of Senior Field Command 400 and Commandant of Vilnius for his leadership during the heavy fighting against Soviet troops. He was promoted to *Generalleutnant* on 30 January 1945 and shortly after receiving his award he was appointed Commandant of Brno in Czechoslovakia. During the final weeks of the war he was appointed Commandant of Olomouc in Moravia. He was captured by Soviet forces on 9 May 1945 in the town of Tabor in Czechoslovakia and was then taken to the Soviet Union, where he was imprisoned. In his capacity as a city commander of Vitebsk, Smolensk, Gomel and Vilna, he was responsible for crimes committed in the field of the occupied Soviet Union, and personally signed the execution orders against fifty Soviet citizens. On 2 November 1946, he was sentenced to death by a Soviet Military Tribunal of the Ivanovskij Garrison in the Moscow military district. A pardon was rejected and he was executed on 8 August 1947 at the Krasnogorsk Prison Camp in the Soviet Union.

Richard Robert Theodor ZIMMER

Generalleutnant

* 21 June 1893, Sschwäbisch Gmünd
+ 20 June 1971, Mittenwald

Knight's Cross: Awarded on 16 October 1944 as *Generalleutnant* and Commander of the 17th Infantry Division for actions in southern Ukraine, where his command suffered heavy casualties, and later saw action defending southern Poland. At the end of September he was appointed Higher Engineer Commander XV. with special duties, with his headquarters in Zell am See in Austria, part of Military District XVIII. Here he became responsible for the expansion of the Reich's defensive position in the mountainous region of Styria in southern Austria. He surrendered to the Allies in Austria on 8 May 1945 and was released after only a few weeks and returned to Germany.

Richard Zimmer joined the Army as a war volunteer in August 1914 and served with the searchlight platoon of XIII. Army Corps. He was commissioned as a *Leutnant* in December 1917. He joined the *Landespolizei* after the war and from October 1933 he served in the Württemberg Ministry of the Interior. In October 1935 he transferred back into the Army with the rank of *Major* and joined Engineer Battalion 5 in Ulm. Later he was appointed company commander with Engineer Battalion 25. In November 1938, now with the rank of *Oberstleutnant*, he was commander of Mountain Engineer Battalion of the 1st Mountain Division, seeing action in France and then patrolling the Swiss border with Germany. From May 1940 he served as commander of training at the Engineer School at Dessau-Rosslau and in April 1943 he took command of the 17th Infantry Division, now with the rank of *Generalmajor*. He was promoted to *Generalleutnant* in January 1944.

Fritz-Georg Hugo Karl von RAPPARD

Generalleutnant

* 15 August 1892, Sögeln, Bersenbrück
+ 29 January 1946, Velikije-Luki, Soviet Union

Knight's Cross: Awarded on 20 October 1944 as *Generalleutnant* and Commander of the 7th Infantry Division for his leadership during the defensive actions, which could be described as a fighting retreat, along the Lower Narew and Bug Rivers in Poland. On 25 August, during heavy fighting behind the Bug River, he led

Fritz-Georg von Rappard entered the Army with Jäger Battalion 7 in March 1911 and served with this unit throughout the First World War. He served with the 18th Infantry Regiment until May 1927, when he transferred as company commander of the 6th Infantry Regiment and was promoted to *Hauptmann* in February 1928. From May 1935 he served as an instructor at the Infantry School in Döberitz and was promoted to *Oberstleutnant* in August 1937. He was attached to the 277th Infantry Regiment at the outbreak of the Second World War, now with the rank of *Oberst*. He took over the leadership of the 83rd Infantry Division from February 1942 and was promoted to *Generalmajor* in November, when he took command of the 7th Infantry Division.

his division during an outstanding defensive action near Wywłóka and Turzyn near the city of Szczecin, Poland.

Knight's Cross with Oakleaves: He became the 751st recipient on 24 February 1945 as *Generalleutnant* and still Commander of the 7th Infantry Division for his outstanding leadership during the defensive actions between 14 and 15 January, during which time his command destroyed almost fifty Soviet tanks, and by the 16th they had destroyed 120 tanks. Rappard led his troops tirelessly day and night, pushing back the Soviet counter-attacks and preventing an enemy breakthrough in the area around Danzig. During the last weeks of the war Rappard saw action in East Prussia, where he surrendered to Soviet troops on 10 May 1945. He was imprisoned and tried as a war criminal for crimes committed against Soviet partisans and as a result he was found guilty and sentenced to death by hanging. The sentence was carried out in Velikije Luki Prison on 29 January 1946.

Werner Rudolf Alfred Fedor von BERCKEN

Generalleutnant

* 8 February 1897, Oppeln, Silesia
+ 29 February 1976, Röttgen near Bonn, North Rhine-Westphalia

Knight's Cross: Awarded on 23 October 1944 as *Generalleutnant* and Commander of the 102nd Infantry Division, part of the I. Cavalry Corps, for his distinguished leadership of his division near Novgorod, on the Narew River, where his troops repeatedly denied the efforts of the Soviet 47th Army to achieve a crossing. He was promoted to *Generalleutnant* in August 1944, continuing to oversee his troops during the fighting on the Eastern Front and by February 1945 his command was operating in the *Heiligenbeil* or East Prussian Pocket. On 5 April he was transferred and appointed Commander of the 558th *Volksgrenadier* Division, where he fought at Pillau and his command suffered heavy casualties. Bercken and the remnants of his command surrendered to Soviet troops on 28 April and he remained in Soviet captivity until 10 October 1955, when a general amnesty was issued.

Herbert WAGNER
Generalleutnant

* 19 January 1896, Stuttgart, Württemberg
+ 5 September 1968, Rommelshausen, Baden-Württemberg

Knight's Cross: Awarded on 23 October 1944 as *Generalleutnant* and Commander of the 132nd Infantry Division for actions in Riga and Latvia as part of Army Group North. He took part in the fighting in the Courland Pocket, where his command suffered heavy losses and as a result the division's Grenadier Regiment 437 had to be disbanded. From 8 January 1945 Wagner became Higher Artillery Commander 302 while attached to the 4th Army until April 1945, when the remaining staff together with staff from *Steiner* Army Group were merged and became the 21st Army. By May his command had marched towards the Western Allies and on 2 May he surrendered to British troops. Wagner remained in Allied captivity until 25 September 1947, when he returned to Germany.

Karl Hans Maximilian von LE SUIRE
General der Gebirgstruppe

* 8 November 1898, Unterwössen, Traunstein
+ 18 June 1954, Stalingrad hospital

Knight's Cross: Awarded on 26 November 1944 as *General der Gebirgstruppe* and Commanding General of the XXXXIX. Mountain Army Corps for his leadership while defending against a Soviet offensive on the Carpathian front on the Eastern Front. The Soviet offensive began in September 1944 and German forces were consistently able to push back enemy forces. After five weeks of hard fighting the Soviet offensive was suspended and Le Suire was awarded the Knight's Cross for the major role he played and for his tactical and operational talents that led to the victory. By the beginning of 1945, however, his command was retreating through the High Tatras Slovakian mountain area towards Upper Silesia. In May 1945 Le Suire surrendered his command to Soviet forces east of Prague and was held prisoner until his death in a hospital near Stalingrad in June 1954. His body was later released and returned to Germany, and he is buried today in Parish Cemetery in Unterwössen, Bavaria.

Karl von Le Suire [left], seen here with Willy Nagel, entered the Bavarian Infantry Regiment in December 1916, seeing action until he was wounded in July 1918. At the end of the war he joined the *Freikorps* as a *Leutnant* and entered the Weapon School at Dresden in April 1925. He was promoted to *Oberleutnant* three months later. He entered the War Academy as an instructor from October 1934 and five years later, now with the rank of *Oberstleutnant*, he was appointed Chief of Operations on the General Staff of the 30th Infantry Division, seeing action in Poland. From June 1940 he served on the General Staff of Mountain Corps Norwegen and was promoted to *Oberst* in December 1941. He was appointed Commander of Jäger Regiment 99 in September 1942. He later took over the leadership of the 46th Infantry Division and later the 117th Jäger Division.

Hans Karl August BOECKH-BEHRENS
Generalleutnant

* 27 November 1898, Wernigerode, Saxony
+ 13 February 1955, Vojkovo Prison Camp No. 48, Soviet Union

Knight's Cross: Awarded on 9 December 1944 as *Generalleutnant* and Commander of the 32nd Infantry Division while attached to the II. Army Corps for action during the fighting in the Skrunda area near Latvia. On 2 November

Hans Boeckh-Behrens entered the Army in October 1914 and was attached to Infantry Regiment 36. In January 1915 he was promoted to *Leutnant* and appointed company officer. He was taken prisoner by the French in May 1917 and was released three years later and returned to Germany, where he remained in the army. He served with the *Reichswehr* in Rifle Regiment 8 and later with Infantry Regiment 17 and attended various courses. By October 1935 he was serving as a company officer with the rank of *Hauptmann*. From August 1936 until July 1939 he served as tactics instructor at the War Academy and at the start of the Second World War he was Chief of the General Staff of the Special Purpose Corps Command with the rank of *Oberstleutnant*. He later served in a similar position with the 16th Army and from January 1942 he served as Chief of the General Staff of the 16th Army with the rank of *Oberst*.

1944 the Soviets broke through the German defences and advanced on the German position but were pushed back and unable to make another attack. At the middle of January 1945 Boeckh-Behrens saw action on the northern sector after Soviet forces broke the siege of Leningrad and his division was cited for its excellent conduct during the retreat through the Baltic States. Boeckh-Behrens, together with his division, was evacuated by sea and was later cut off on the Hela Peninsula by Soviet forces. It was there that he surrendered and he was imprisoned by the Soviets in Vojkovo prison camp, where he died in February 1955.

Wilhelm HEUN

Generalleutnant

* 23 May 1895, Herborn, Hesse-Nassau
\+ 21 September 1986, Göttingen, Lower Saxony

Knight's Cross: Awarded on 9 December 1944 as *Generalmajor* and Commander of the 83rd Infantry Division in recognition of his success during the decisive counter-attack near Riteli in the Courland area on 6 November 1944. At 0900 on 6 November 1944, Soviet forces attacked Heun's division with far superior forces and very quickly secured a commanding position. Heun then brought up his available reserves and prepared them for a concentrated attack, which they implemented with great skill and the Soviet forces that had broken through were virtually destroyed. As a result the Soviets decided to suspend their offensive. Heun continued against the Soviet army on the Eastern Front

Wilhelm Heun studied civil engineering in Darmstadt from April 1914 and entered the Army Reserves as a war volunteer in August of that year. He was commissioned as a *Leutnant der Reserve* in May 1916 and served as a platoon leader in the 2nd Company of Infantry Regiment 28 from June. He left the Army at the end of the war and continued with his civil engineering studies at technical college, rejoining in May 1934 with the rank of *Hauptman*. He took command of various companies and from August 1939, now with the rank of *Major*, he took command of the I. Battalion of Infantry Regiment 161. From May 1940 he saw action in France and from June 1941 he fought in the Soviet Union. He later took command of Infantry Regiment 435 and was promoted to *Generalmajor* in May 1944 as commander of the 83rd Infantry Division.

and in the Soviet Union, seeing more action in the Courland area before being relieved in March 1945 for some rest. In April he took command of the 1st RAD Division Schlageter, which had been formed from 7,500 men of the Reich Labour Service, and they were deployed near Waren in Mecklenburg-Vorpommern as part of the 3rd Panzer Army. Heun surrendered his division to American troops on 3 May 1945.

Max-Josef Johann PEMSEL

Generalleutnant

* 15 January 1897, Regensburg
+ 30 June 1985, Munich

Max-Josef Pemsel entered the Army as a war volunteer in April 1916 and served with the Royal Bavarian 11th Reserve Infantry Regiment. He was promoted to *Leutnant* in April 1918 and served as a battalion commander, remaining in the Army after the war. He served with the 11th and 48th Infantry Regiments and attended a military ski in March 1920. He later served with Infantry Regiment 20 and by April 1933 had been promoted to the rank of *Hauptmann*.

Knight's Cross: Awarded on 9 December 1944 as *Generalmajor* and Commander of the 6th Mountain Division for his leadership during the fierce rearguard battles during the German retreat from northern Finland from

Pemsel, seen here with *Generalfeldmarschall* Wilhelm List. From September 1935 he was Chief of Operations of the Mountain Brigade in Munich, which by the beginning of the war had become the 1st Mountain Division. From October 1939, now with the rank of *Oberstleutnant i.G.*, he served as Chief of Operations on the General Staff of the XVIII. Army Corps, which later became a Mountain Corps. From October he was Chief of the General Staff of the XVIII. Mountain Corps, seeing action in Bulgaria, Greece and later Lapland. In June 1943 he was appointed Chief of the General Staff of the 7th Army, seeing action on the western Atlantic coast, and he was promoted to *Generalmajor* in September 1943.

early October 1944. During the heavy fighting he personally saw to it that an attack by the Soviet Army against the XIX. Mountain Army Corps failed and that the Petsame–Kirkenes Road was reopened. Shortly after on 15 December Pemsel was promoted to the rank of *Generalleutnant* and continued to command his division during the retreat across Lapland in April 1945. From 10 April Pemsel served as Chief of the General Staff of Army *Ligurian* under the command of the Italian *Marshal* Rodolfo Graziani, seeing action in Italy. Pemsel was captured by the Allies in the area of Lake Como in Italy on 29 April 1945 and was held as a prisoner of war by the Americans and later the British. He was released from captivity on 29 April 1948 and returned to Germany. In April 1956 he entered the *Bundeswehr*, where he served until September 1961. He was military consultant to the makers of the 1962 film *The Longest Day*, in which he was portrayed by Wolfgang Preiss.

Hermann Bruno SCHATZ

Generalmajor

* 26 June 1894, Markneukirchen, Oelsnitz
+ 3 December 1974, Murnau, Garmisch-Partenkirchen

Knight's Cross: Awarded on 9 December 1944 as *Oberst* and Commander of Grenadier Regiment 977, while attached to the 271st *Volksgrenadier* Division for actions in the southern sector of the Eastern Front. He saw action in the city of Székesfehérvár in Hungary, where he led his regiment with great skill

Bruno Schatz was a war volunteer in February 1915 and served with the Royal Saxony Infantry Regiment No. 133. He was commissioned as a *Leutnant* in December of that year. He left the Army in December 1919, having won the Iron Cross 1st and 2nd Classes. He was employed as a State Border Guard until October 1935, when he returned to the Army with the rank of *Hauptmann*. He served as a company commander at the Army NCO School at Potsdam from October 1936 and from November 1938 he served as tactics instructor. In November 1939 he was battalion commander with Infantry Regiment 31, seeing action in Poland, and from May 1940 he fought in France, now with the rank of *Oberstleutnant*. From August 1941 he served as Commander of Infantry Regiment 261 and saw action in the Soviet Union until December 1942, when he was attached to the Infantry School in Döberitz.

and courage. He later saw action in Budapest, where he was given the leadership of the 122nd Infantry Division, seeing action in the Courland Pocket, and where in April 1945 his command was confirmed when he was promoted to *Generalmajor*. He surrendered to Soviet troops on 8 May 1945 in the Courland area and was convicted of being a war criminal. He spent several years in various prison camps until his release under a general amnesty in October 1955, when he returned to Germany.

Heribert Adolf Karl Arthur von LARISCH

Generalleutnant

* 18 July 1894, Freiburg im B
+ 20 March 1952, Hamburg

Knight's Cross: Awarded on 26 December 1944 as *Generalleutnant* and Commander of the 129th Infantry Division for his defence of the Narew River, a tributary of the River Vistula, against a strong Soviet assault. In June that year the Soviets had launched a massive offensive known as Operation Bagration and while his infantry division escaped total decimation like many of the units attached to Army Group Centre, they suffered heavy losses. The German units had set up strong defences along the river, including trenches, barbed wire and minefields, which managed to prevent the Soviets breaking through. In January 1945, during another large-scale Soviet offensive, the German defensive line at the Narew was overrun. Winter temperatures had caused the marshes to

Heribert von Larisch entered the Army in February 1914 with Dragoon Regiment 18 and seven months later he was commissioned as a *Leutnant*. When the First World War ended he stayed with the Army, serving as an infantry leader and an instructor at the Infantry School in Döberitz. From October 1937 he served as a tactics instructor at the War School in Hannover with the rank of *Major*. He served as a battalion commander with Infantry Regiment 440 from January 1940 and was promoted to the rank of *Oberst* in October 1941. From November 1942 he served as commander of Fortress Brigade 1 in Salonika and that same month he was also commander of the German Railway Security Staff in Croatia. In July 1943 he attended the 6th Divisional Leaders' Course in Berlin and took command of the 78th Assault Division a few months later.

freeze, making the terrain impermeable to attack but the line was smashed and German units were forced to retreat. By then his infantry division had suffered such heavy losses that it basically ceased to exist and Larisch gave up command on 15 February 1945. For the rest of the war he was posted as commander of Infantry School Döberitz and remained in that position until 24 April, when he was placed in the Reserves. After the war Larisch was able to evade capture until 15 June 1945, when he was arrested by an American patrol and spent the next two years as a prisoner, being released in July 1947.

Mauritz Egon Kurt Freiherr von STRACHWITZ UND GROSS ZAUCHE

Generalleutnant

* 12 October 1898, Bruschewitz, Trebnitz
+ 10 December 1953, a Prison Soviet Camp in Asbest near Sverdlovsk

Knight's Cross: Awarded on 9 January 1945 as *Generalleutnant* and Commander of the 87th Infantry Division, part of the 18th Army, for actions during the retreat through the Baltic States and the battles in the Courland Pocket. The fighting in the Courland area became more and more intense and by April 1945 the Soviets had virtually destroyed most of the division and its 185th Grenadier Regiment had been disbanded. On 9 May Strachwitz und Gross Zauche surrendered to the Soviets and a Soviet Military Court in Vitebsk sentenced him to twenty-five years' imprisonment on 18 August 1948. The conditions were terrible and as a result he died on 23 October 1955. He has no grave.

Mauritz von Strachwitz und Gross Zauche joined the Army in July 1916 and was commissioned as a *Leutnant* in December 1917. He later served as a platoon leader and an ordnance officer and stayed in the army after the war, being promoted to *Rittmeister* in April 1933. By August 1936 he was Squadron Chief with the 8th Cavalry Regiment in Breslau with the rank of *Major*, and later served on the staff of the Inspector of Cavalry. From March 1938 he was Chief of Operations of the 18th Infantry Division. He later served as Chief of Operations of the VIII. Army Corps and then in a similar position with the 18th Army under *Generaloberst* Georg Küchler. Promoted to *Oberst* in January 1942, he became Chief of the General Staff of the X. Army Corps later that year and from November 1943 he took command of the 87th Infantry Division.

Josef Otto Gerhard PRINNER

Generalleutnant

* 18 December 1894, Munich, Bavaria
+ 1 July 1964, Munich, Bavaria

Knight's Cross: Awarded on 11 January 1945 as *Generalleutnant* and Higher Artillery Commander 311 for actions in the Carpathian Forests on the Eastern Front as part of the Panzer Group 1. During the last days of the war he managed to retreat with his command towards the Western Allies. He surrendered to US troops on 9 May 1945 and remained in Allied captivity until June 1947.

Josef Prinner entered the Army with the 5th Company of Fusilier Artillery Regiment 1 in July 1914 and was commissioned as a *Leutnant* in December. He served as a regimental adjutant from November 1917 and was promoted to *Oberleutnant* in July 1918. In October 1935 he transferred back into the Army and was appointed Commander of I. Battalion of Artillery Regiment 41 in Ulm from October 1936. He served as commander of Artillery Staff Regiment 697 from August 1939 and was promoted to *Oberst* in September 1940. Two months later he transferred into Artillery Regiment 81. Promoted to *Generalmajor* in March 1943, he served as commander of the 340th Infantry Division until October that year, when he attended the 6th Divisional Leaders' Course. From November 1943 he became High Artillery Commander 311 on the Eastern Front

Ferdinand Alfred Friedrich JODL

General der Gebirgstruppe

* 28 November 1896, Landau, Bavaria
+ 9 June 1956, Essen, North Rhine-Westphalia

Knight's Cross: Awarded on 13 January 1945 as *General der Gebirgstruppe* and Commanding General of the XIX. Mountain Corps for his distinguished command during the defensive battles against a superior enemy near Petsamo in Finland. Jodl was a careful, almost cautious, leader, especially against enemy forces that were five times superior in number. After Finland's capitulation, his mountain corps had the difficult task of securing the flanks of the German

Ferdinand Jodl [left) was the brother of Alfred Jodl [right], Chief of Operations Staff with the High Command of the Wehrmacht. He entered the Army in August 1914 with Bavarian Field Artillery Regiment 4, seeing action during the First World War. He was commissioned as a *Leutnant* in November 1915 while serving as a battery officer with the 3rd Battery of his regiment. He remained with the Army after the war and by August 1935 he had been promoted to *Hauptmann* and was serving as tactics instructor at the War Academy. From 1938 he served as Chief of Operations on the General Staff of the XII. Army Corps and was promoted to *Oberstleutnant* in January 1939. From June 1940 he took up the same position with the XXXIX. Mountain Corps. From January 1942 Jodl saw action in Norway and then in Lapland, and was promoted to *Generalleutnant* in September 1943. From April 1944 he was commander of the XIX. Mountain Corps, and was promoted to *General der Gebirgstruppe* in September 1944.

units that were retreating from the area around Kandalaksha. However, Jodl did successfully complete the withdrawal of the troops under his command from the area behind the Lyngen Fjord in Norway, despite the danger from enemy fighter aircraft, artillery and snipers. He ended the war as commander of German forces in North Norway, grouped under the name Army Detachment *Narvik*. He surrendered to Allied troops on 9 May 1945 and remained in captivity until his release in July 1947.

Karl RÜBEL

Generalleutnant

* 16 August 1895, Dortmund, Westphalia
+ 8 March 1945, Świdwin, Pomerania

Karl Rübel entered the Army as a *Fahnenjunker* in March 1914 and was commissioned as a *Leutnant* nine months later. He served as a company leader from March 1915 and then as an adjutant with the III. Battalion of Infantry Regiment 56. Promoted to *Oberleutnant* in October 1918, he briefly joined the *Freikorps* in May 1919 and then rejoined the Army and served with Infantry Regiments 7 and 10. From October 1934 he commanded the Army Sports School in Wünsdorf and in November 1938, now with the rank of *Oberstleutnant*, he was battalion commander with Infantry Regiment 57. At the outbreak of war in September 1939 he was commander of Infantry Replacement Regiment 251 in Friedberg and then a few months later took command of Infantry Regiment 378. Promoted to *Oberst* in July 1940, he took command of the 163rd Infantry Division from December 1942 and saw action on the Eastern Front.

Knight's Cross: Awarded on 13 January 1945 as *Generalleutnant* and Commander of the 163rd Infantry Division for actions in the Baltic area and during the defence of Kolberg, where his command put up a desperate resistance. On 8 March the Soviets finally stormed the city and the 163rd Infantry Division was virtually destroyed. Rübel was killed in Świdwin, Pomerania, and is believed to have been buried in the German War Cemetery in Stare Czarnowo, Poland.

Erhard-Heinrich BERNER

Generalmajor

* 12 September 1894, Schellerhau, Saxony
+ 25 July 1960, Hannover-Linden, Lower Saxony

Knight's Cross: Awarded on 18 January 1943 as *Oberst* and Commander of *Jäger* Regiment 28, part of the 8th Jäger Division, in recognition of his leadership during the fighting in the Demjansk area of the Eastern Front. He later led his regiment during the fighting in the Demjansk area as part of the 8th *Jäger*

Division and continued to see action on the northern sector of the Eastern Front until after the retreat from Leningrad. He had been promoted to *Oberst* in December 1943 and in March 1944 led his regiment on the southern sector of the front, seeing action during the retreat through Ukraine, the Carpathians and Slovakia. In February 1945 Berner was delegated with the leadership of the 76th Infantry Division and continued to see action in Slovakia. On 20 April he was promoted to *Generalmajor* and confirmed as divisional commander. By now, however, due to the heavy fighting and the amount of casualties, his command had been reduced from a division to a battle group and, together with the 1st Panzer Army, was surrounded by the Soviets. Berner surrendered in May, spending the next ten years in a Soviet prison camp.

Eberhard Franz THUNERT

Generalmajor

* 23 November 1899, Kulmsee, Kulm
\+ 4 May 1964, Wuppertal

Knight's Cross: Awarded on 1 February 1945 as *Generalmajor* and Commander of the 1st Panzer Division while attached to the 6th Army, he managed to lead his division and other German units out of encirclement at Lake Balaton in Hungary, which lasted until March. Thunert then led his division across the Danube and they fought a strong Soviet force from the Demyansk Pocket to the Reich border by early April. He then led his division away from the

Eberhard Thunert entered the Army in March 1918 and was in the field three months later with the 7th Company of Infantry Regiment 61. He remained in the Army after the war and was commissioned as a *Leutnant* in April 1922 as company commander with Infantry Regiment 6. In October 1935 he served as Second General Staff Officer with the 12th Division with the rank of *Hauptmann* and from November 1938 served as Chief of Operations on the General Staff of the 5th Panzer Division, seeing action during the French campaign. In September he served in a similar position with the XIV. Army Corps, fighting on the Eastern Front from June 1941 and now with the rank of *Oberstleutnant*. In August 1942 he was wounded at Stalingrad and flown out of the city. Once recovered he served as Chief of the General Staff of the new XIV. Panzer Corps, now with the rank of *Oberst*.

Red Army and fought in the Hartberg area in Styria, Austria, and from there marched towards the American lines at Mauerkirchen in Upper Bavaria, where he surrendered his troops to the Americans. Most of his soldiers were released and sent home by late July and Thunert was kept in prison until August 1947, when he returned home.

Dr med. dent. Walter Karl Friedrich ASSMANN

Generalleutnant

* 3 June 1896, Mühlhausen, north-east of Thüringen
+ 1 May 1964, Offenbach, Hesse

Knight's Cross: Awarded on 10 February 1945 as *Generalmajor* and Commander of the 101st *Jäger* Division, part of the XXXIX. Mountain *Jäger* Corps, for distinguished service in battle. He saw action during the defensive fighting between 16 and 27 July 1944 south of Banská Štiavnica in Slovakia and during the fighting in the Grand Valley. In February 1945 his division was in the Javornik or Maple Mountains in Czechoslovakia. It formed the rearguard for the XLVI. Panzer Corps during the breakout of the Kamenets–Podolsky Pocket while retreating across Ukraine. On 16 March 1945 Assmann was promoted to *Generalleutnant* and shortly before the end of the war, after bitter fighting across Slovakia, Hungary, Ukraine and Austria, his command had been reduced to the size of a battle group. Assmann surrendered to American troops on 9 May 1945, being held in captivity until 25 June 1947.

Walter Assmann entered military service as a war volunteer on 10 August 1914, and was commissioned as a *Leutnant* in January 1915. From August he served as a platoon leader. In April 1917 he served as temporary adjutant of 102nd Reserve Infantry Brigade and remained in the Army until January 1920. He rejoined fourteen years later and in 1940 saw action during the French campaign, when he was wounded during an attack near the Maginot Line. He continued to see action during the Western campaign until 22 June 1941, when his regiment took part in the invasion of the Soviet Union.

Rudolf August Friedrich Georg SPERL

Generalleutnant

* 11 October 1898, Allenstein
+ 23 August 1981, Bad Rappenau

Knight's Cross: Awarded on 10 February 1945 as *Generalleutnant* and Commander of the 61st *Volksgrenadier* Division for actions near Königsberg in East Prussia, where the unit served at battle group strength until 10 April 1945. On that date Königsberg was overrun by the Soviets and Sperls' 61st division was destroyed. He was taken prisoner and kept in Soviet captivity until a general amnesty in October 1955, when he returned to Germany.

Rudolf Sperl transferred into Field Artillery Regiment 58 from the Cadet School in March 1916 and was commissioned as a *Leutnant* in January 1917. He joined the *Freikorps* after the war before rejoining the Army in January 1921. By October 1935, with the rank of *Hauptmann*, he became company commander with Artillery Regiment 18 in Glogau before being assigned to the General Staff of the Army from November 1936. Promoted to *Oberstleutnant* in April 1939, he became Chief of Operations of the 35th Infantry Division at the start of the Second World War. From October 1940 he served as Chief of the General Staff of the L. Army Corps under the command of General der Kavallerie Georg Lindemann, seeing action in the Soviet Union from June 1941. He later attended the 8th regimental Course and was appointed commander of the 15th Infantry Division in November 1943 before becoming commander of the 61st Volksgrenadier Division from December 1944.

Leonhard Julius Siegfried HASS

Generalleutnant

* 7 June 1898, Burg, Solingen
+ 14 December 1987, Nordhorn

Knight's Cross: Awarded on 18 February 1945 as *Generalleutnant* and Commander of the 170th Infantry Division, part of the 18th Army, for actions on the Eastern Front. Hass led his division during some tough and costly defensive battles from mid-January 1945. He withdrew his division in the direction of Königsberg, where it was surrounded with other units of the German 4th Army.

Siegfried Hass entered the Army with Replacement Jäger Battalion 1 Graf Yorck von Wartenburg in August 1916 and was taken ill in August 1917. He returned to the front line in November but was seriously wounded in June 1918. In October 1919 he transferred into the *Reichswehr* and attended various courses in Munich, Döberitz and Jüterborg before being promoted to *Hauptmann* in April 1933. In October 1935 he was appointed commander of the 13th Company with Infantry Regiment 44 and in March 1938 he took over as battalion commander with Infantry Regiment 57. He was promoted to the rank of *Oberstleutnant* in April 1940. He saw action during the invasion of France in May 1940 and from June the following year took part in the invasion of the Soviet Union.

At the end of January his division, together with other divisions from the 4th Army, tried to break through from East into West Prussia, but this failed. As a result, his division was trapped in the Heiligenbeil Pocket during the closing stages of the war and was almost destroyed during the Soviet Braunsberg Offensive Operation of 13–22 March 1945. Soviet forces claimed 93,000 dead in the area and took more than 46,000 soldiers prisoner but Hass and survivors from his division managed to escape the clutches of the Red Army and surrendered to British troops on 11 May 1945.

Wolf-Dietrich Ritter und Edler von XYLANDER

Generalleutnant

* 9 April 1903, Munich
+ 15 February 1945 near Struppen, Pirna

Wolf-Dietrich Ritter und Edler von Xylander entered the Army in May 1921 with the training battalion of Infantry Regiment 19 and was commissioned as a *Leutnant* in March 1925. He continued to serve in the same regiment for the next twelve years and trained as a General Staff Officer. He was promoted to *Major* in March 1939 and from June 1940 served as Chief of Operations on the Staff of the 30th Infantry Division, seeing action in France. In August 1941 he served as Chief of Operations with the 2nd Army, fighting on the Eastern Front, and was promoted to *Oberstleutnant* in September. He was appointed Chief of the General Staff of the XXXIX. Mountain Corps in January 1943 and six months later was appointed Chief of the General Staff of the 17th Army. He was promoted to *Generalmajor* in January 1944.

Knight's Cross: Awarded posthumously on 20 February 1945 as *Generalleutnant* and Chief of the General Staff of Army Group Centre for his leadership and bravery during the Kuban Bridgehead crisis in the Crimea. He flew a considerable distance over enemy occupied territory in order to deliver an important message to another Army Group, and after being told of the situation he made his own decision and sent the unit back on a successful attack on a Soviet armoured force that had crossed the Oder. On 15 February 1945 General Xylander was killed when his courier aircraft, a Heinkel He 111, was shot down when it ran into an Allied air attack over Dresden. He is buried today at the War Cemetery in Munich Row 100, Grave No. 14.

Siegfried Leopold Friedrich REIN

Generalleutnant

* 3 August 1894, Schernfeld, Eichstätt
+ 16 January 1945, Königsberg, East Prussia

Knight's Cross: Awarded posthumously on 24 February 1945 as *Generalleutnant* and Commander of the 69th Infantry Division for his leadership during the heavy fighting during the Battle of Tilsit and additional action on the Russian Front. He received the following assessment from *General der Infantry* Gerhard Matzky, Commanding General of the XXVI. Army Corps, 'Generalleutnant Siegfried Rein was a very conscientious soldier who acted clearly and determined ... and proved himself mentally strong in a crisis ...' He was killed in action in

Siegfried Rein entered the Army in October 1913 and was commissioned as a *Leutnant* twelve months later, seeing action in the First World War with Army Telephone Battalion 6. He ended the war as an *Oberleutnant* and joined the *Freikorps von Epp* in April 1919. He later entered the *Reichswehr* and was assigned to the Reich Defence Ministry in July 1933, being promoted to *Major* the following year. From August 1939 he was commander of Army Signals Regiment 563 in Münster and was promoted to *Oberst* in March 1940. From August he was Army Signals Leader with the 18th Army, seeing action on the Eastern Front, and from June 1942 he was transferred and became the commander of the Army Signals School in Halle. Promoted to *Generalmajor* in September 1943, he later attended the 8th Divisional Leaders' Course before being appointed commander of the 69th Infantry Division in February 1944.

Königsberg in January 1945 together with many of his command, and later in April the majority of his remaining command was destroyed and those who survived the Soviet onslaught were taken prisoner.

Siegfried Julius Theodor VERHEIN

Generalleutnant

* 1 October 1897, Gahlkow, Pomerania
+ 30 June 1963, Mainz, Rhineland-Palatinate

Knight's Cross: Awarded on 28 February 1945 as *Generalmajor* and Commander of Battle Group 551 of the *Volksgrenadier* Division for actions on the Eastern Front and particularly in East Prussia. On 20 April he was promoted to the rank of *Generalleutnant* and saw action during the Battle of Tilsit. His command was later cut off in the Samland–Danzig area when caught out by the sudden and rapid advance of the Red Army into north-eastern Germany. He was wounded on 19 April, but not seriously, and from the 24th he took over command of the 28th *Jäger* Division, ending the war in East Prussia, where he surrendered to Soviet troops. In July 1949 Verhein was sentenced to twenty-five years' hard labour by a Military Tribunal in Novgorod and spent time in various prison camps including No. 27 Krasnogorsk, No. 48 Černy, Ležnevo, No. 270 Boroviči and No. 144 Vorošilovgrad. He was finally released from Soviet captivity on 8 October 1955 and returned to Germany.

Siegfried Verhein entered the Army in July 1915 with Field Artillery 38, being commissioned as a *Leutnant* in September 1916, and was awarded both classes of the Iron Cross. He stayed in the Army until July 1930 and rejoined three years later. He was promoted to *Hauptmann* in May 1934 and appointed battery commander with Artillery Regiment 2 the following year. From October 1936 he served as tactics instructor at the War School in Dresden and from September 1939 he was attached to the Personnel Office of the Army High Command. From March 1941 he was Head of Department 4 (Artillery) in the Army Personnel Office with the rank of *Oberstleutnant* and from June 1943 he was Commander of Artillery Regiment 32.

Kurt HAEHLING

Generalmajor

* 7 November 1897, Rosengarten, East Prussia
+ 20 May 1983, Finsterwalde, Brandenburg

Kurt Haehling entered the Army as a war volunteer in August 1914 and was attached to Field Artillery Regiment 52 until October 1915, when he transferred into Field Artillery Regiment 97. He left the Army in 1920 and joined the police, rising to the rank of *Polizei-Hauptmann* in January 1935 and later that year he rejoined the army. He was attached to the I. Battalion of Artillery Regiment 47 with the rank of *Hauptmann* and attended various courses before taking over command of the III. Battalion of Artillery Regiment 1. He was promoted to *Oberstleutnant* in November 1940 and from January 1941 he took command of Artillery Regiment 294. He was promoted to *Oberst* in June 1942. A year later Haehling was appointed Artillery Commander 108 and after attending a divisional leaders' course in May 1944 he was given the leadership of the 73rd Infantry Division two months later. He was promoted to *Generalmajor* in January 1945.

Knight's Cross: Awarded on 2 March 1945 as *Generalmajor* and Commander of the 126th Infantry Division, part of the 18th Army, under *General der Infanterie* Ehrenfried-Oskar Boege for actions in the Baltic States and later in the Courland area. He led his division during six battles in the Courland and on 8 May he surrendered to Soviet troops in the Libau area together with more than 3,000 soldiers, of which seventy were officers. He was released from Soviet captivity in March 1951 and returned to Germany.

Werner Karl Otto Leopold RANCK

Generalleutnant

* 25 October 1904, Hamburg
+ 7 December 1989, Hamburg

Knight's Cross: Awarded on 2 March 1945 as *Generalmajor* and Commander of the 121st Infantry Division for actions during the retreat from Leningrad through the Baltic States and during the retreat to the western coast of Latvia. On 20 April 1945 he was promoted to *Generalleutnant* and from 1 May he took

Werner Ranck was commissioned as a *Leutnant* with Artillery Regiment 6 in December 1927 and served with this regiment until October 1934. A year later he was commander of the 3rd Battery of Artillery Regiment in Münster with the rank of *Hauptmann* and the following year he attended the War Academy in Berlin. At the outbreak of the Second World War he was serving as Chief of Operations of the 93rd Infantry Division and form February 1940 he was Chief of Operations of the 15th Infantry Division. From May 1940 Ranck saw action in France and was promoted to *Major* in October. From January 1941 he served as Chief of Intelligence with the 11th Army, seeing action in the Soviet Union from June of that year. He later served as Chief of Operations with the 290th Infantry Division and from December 1943 he was Chief of the General Staff of the X. Army Corps. From September 1944 he served as leader of the 121st Infantry Division. over as Commander of the 218th Infantry Division in the Courland Pocket. There, on 9 May, he surrendered to Soviet forces. Ranck was imprisoned in the NKWD Camp No. 3 in Ukraine and later moved to various different camps, including No. 27, Krasnogorsk, Camp No. 48 Černcy, Ležnevo, Camp No. 5 near Rakvere and Camp No. 1 in Tallinn. In December 1949 he was tried by a Soviet Military Court and sentenced to twenty-five years' hard labour, together with *Generalleutnant* Wilhelm Ochsner and *Generalleutnant* Erich Reuter, and they were released after a general amnesty in October 1955.

Wilhelm Ernst PHILIPPS

Generalleutnant

* 29 July 1894, Wuppertal-Barmen
+ 13 February 1971, Esslingen

Knight's Cross: Awarded on 5 March 1945 as *Generalleutnant* and Commander of the 3rd Panzer Division while attached to Army Group *Balck* for actions during the Dnieper campaign, where he and his division distinguished themselves in Hungary and the Eastern Front. During this time he had been reassigned and was serving as Head of the Department of Armour, Weapons and Equipment with the *Wehrmacht*. He was taken prisoner by American forces on 8 May 1945, and remained in Allied captivity until his release on 22 May 1947.

Wilhelm Philipps entered the Army in March 1913 and served throughout the First World War as a battery leader, battalion leader and regimental adjutant, rising to the rank of *Oberleutnant*. He stayed in the Army after the war and was an expert on military vehicles. From 1927 he commanded a technical college in Dresden. From 1934 he was assigned to the Reich Defence Ministry, now with the rank of *Oberstleutnant*. At the beginning of the Second World War he served as commander of the 11th Panzer Regiment and from February 1940 he was head of the Department of Armour, Weapons and Equipment in the Army. In 1944 he attended a divisional leaders' course and trained as a Panzer officer. From May 1944 he took over as commander of the 20th Panzer Division with the rank of *Generalleutnant*.

Heinrich Georg 'Heinz' HAX

Generalmajor

* 24 January 1900, Berlin
+ 1 September 1969, Koblenz, Rhineland-Palatinate

Knight's Cross: Awarded on 8 March 1945 as *Oberst* and Commander of the 8th Panzer Division, part of the XXIV. Army Corps, for his leadership during the Battle of Lauban in Silesia. The Germans pushed the Soviet forces back and on 4 March they had destroyed a total of 230 Soviet tanks after surrounding the Soviet 99th Motorised Corps.

Heinrich Hax entered the Army as war volunteer with the Guards Fusilier Regiment from January 1918 and he remained with the Army after the war. He was commissioned as a *Leutnant* in April 1922 and was later platoon leader in Infantry Regiment 9. He took part in the Olympic Games in Amsterdam in 1928 and achieved fifth place in the pentathlon. From 1935 he was attached to the Army General Staff and in 1936 he took part in the Berlin Olympic Games and won a silver medal in pistol shooting. Promoted to *Oberstleutnant* in April 1939, he served as tactics instructor at the War Academy from October 1940 and later served as 1st General Staff Officer with Army Group A and then Army Group South. Promoted to *Oberst* in August 1942 he was appointed Chief of the General Staff of the LVI. Army Corps in January 1943. He attended the divisional leaders' course in Hirschberg from December 1944, and by April 1945 he had been appointed commander of the 8th Panzer Division.

Knight's Cross with Oakleaves: He became the 843rd recipient on 30 April 1945 as *Generalmajor* and Commander of the 8th Panzer Division, attached to the 1st Panzer Army, for his outstanding bravery and leadership against strong Soviet forces. On 22 March 1945 Hax led his division during a Soviet attack and penetrated a small village, where his troops destroyed numerous tanks. The Soviets launched a series of attacks against the front line held by two German divisions and applied heavy pressure to the flanks of the entire defending corps to bring about the collapse of the front, although this failed. On 6 April elements of the 8th Panzer Division began its own attack and managed to break the enemy resistance, reaching the Oder River. On 15 April Hax led a counter-attack against Soviet forces in the area around Bruno and attacked the enemy from the rear, preventing another breakthrough. On 9 May 1945 Hax was taken prisoner by US troops in Pilsen and was later handed over to the Soviets, where he remained a prisoner until October 1955. On his return to Germany he rejoined the Army, the *Bundeswehr*, and was promoted to the rank of *Generalmajor* in September 1957.

Theodor KRETSCHMER

Generalmajor

* 26 November 1901, Burghaun, Hünfeld
+ 5 December 1986, Burghaun, Hünfeld

Knight's Cross: Awarded on 8 March 1945 as *Oberst* and Leader of the 17th Panzer Division for actions during actions on the Eastern Front, most notably near Baranow in Poland and in Upper Silesia. His command opposed the Soviet drive west of the

Theodor Kretschmer joined the *Freikorps* in 1919 and in January 1921 he joined the Army and served with Infantry Regiment 6, being commissioned as a *Leutnant* three years later. From April 1934 he served as company leader of Motorised Training Command in Ohrdruf and was later attached to the War Academy in Berlin. In September 1937 he was appointed Chief of Operations on the General Staff of the XVI. Army Corps with the rank of *Hauptmann*. From June 1940 he commanded Panzer Detachment 65, and from April the following year he was promoted to *Oberstleutnant*. In May 1942 he was appointed commander of Panzer Regiment 36 and in September he took command of Department 3 in the Army Personnel Office. He was promoted to *Oberst* the following month.

Vistula River in the winter of 1945 and saw action in the disastrous Battle of the Baranov Bridgehead. Kretschmer was promoted to *Generalmajor* on 1 April 1945 and he ended the war in the Deutsch-Brod Pocket east of Prague, Czechoslovakia, and surrendered to Soviet forces on 11 May. He was imprisoned in a Soviet prison camp until his release on 10 November 1955.

Dr med. dent. Rudolf HÜBNER

Generalmajor

* 29 April 1897, Erlenthal, Schildeberg
+ 28 February 1965, Lemgo

Knight's Cross: Awarded on 9 March 1945 as *Generalleutnant* and Commander of Grenadier Regiment 529 for actions near the Heiligenbeil Pocket on the Eastern Front. From 10 March Hübner was appointed personally by Hitler as commander of Special Court Martial West. When the Bridge at Remagen fell into the hands of the Americans, Hübner arrived at the headquarters of Army Group B, tried the officers responsible for not destroying the bridge and ordered their execution. They were taken to a nearby wood and shot in the back of the neck. Commander-in-Chief of Army Group B *Generalfeldmarschall* Walter Model did nothing to prevent the executions. On 28 April Hübner was appointed Commandant of Munich and it was there that he conducted investigations into the case of the Munich Mutineers, some 200 officers and men who wanted to surrender to the Allies but were executed by hanging.

Rudolf Hübner entered the Army on 25 July 1916 as a volunteer in Battalion of Grenadier Regiment 12, seeing action in the field with Infantry Regiment 51 from 1917. He was commissioned as a *Leutnant* in September 1918 and then was attached to an officers' training course when the war ended. He left the Army to train as a dentist and was successful and set up his own practice, then rejoined the Army in June 1935. He took over the command of a battalion from January 1940 and was promoted to *Major* in March that year. From May 1941 he was tactics instructor at Reconnaissance School 2 in Brieg, Silesia. Promoted to *Oberstleutnant* in April 1942, he took over command of Grenadier Regiment 529 and in December that year he was promoted to *Oberst*. From September 1943 he served in the Army Personnel Office and was later appointed Chief of Staff of the National Socialist Guidance Staff of the Army.

On 8 May 1945 he was captured by US troops and later handed over to the British, being released in April 1948. However, a post-war investigation ended in a trial in Koblenz, where he was sentenced to four years' imprisonment. In 1966 the sentences were reviewed at the State Council in Landshut and he was subsequently acquitted of all charges.

Werner Eduard Berthold FROTSCHER

Generalmajor

* 31 December 1894, Kroppenstedt, Saxony-Anhalt
+ 22 May 1959, Badenweiler, Baden-Württemberg

Knight's Cross: Awarded on 11 March 1945 as *Oberst* and Commander of Grenadier Regiment 422 of the 126th Infantry Division for actions in the Courland area in the Soviet Union. On 20 February 1945 the Soviets began a major attack near Priekule in the Courland region of Latvia and Frotscher's regiment, which was located south of the city, was surrounded. The area was declared a fortress and the following night Frotscher and his men commenced a breakout and were successful in reaching friendly territory near Jūlesmuiža in Latvia, where they occupied a new defensive line. His command was pushed back to the west coast of Latvia and remained isolated in the Courland Pocket until the end of the war. On 20 April Frotscher was promoted to the rank of *Generalmajor*. His regiment had a strength of 3,000 men and seventy officers

Werner Frotscher entered Army Service with I. Replacement Battalion of Infantry Regiment 153 in August 1914 and was commissioned as a *Leutnant* in May 1915, serving as a company officer. He was wounded in July 1916 and later that year served as an orderly officer, a court officer and a gas protection officer. He remained in the Army until April 1923 but returned to military service in 1934 as a *Hauptmann* with Infantry Regiment Tübingen. He later commanded a company with Infantry Regiment 109 and was promoted to *Major* in January 1938 before entering the Reserves in September 1939. Towards the end of the year he was named commander of the II. Battalion of Infantry Regiment 29 and from December 1940 he was Commander of Watch Battalion Berlin. Promoted to *Oberstleutnant* in March 1941, he went on to command Fusilier Regiment 270 from September 1942, now with the rank of *Oberst*, seeing action on the Eastern Front.

when it surrendered to the Red Army near Libau on 8 May 1945. However, Frotscher and his regiment had just managed to board one of the last ships heading for the west and thus avoided Soviet captivity.

Franz Christian PHILIPP

Generalleutnant

* 3 September 1893, Michelfeld, Lower Franconia
+ 16 October 1963, Unterleinleiter, Bavaria

Christian Philipp entered the Army as a war volunteer in August 1914 and served with the 3rd Royal Bavarian Field Artillery Regiment, being promoted to *Leutnant* in December 1915. He joined the *Freikorps* after the war and from December 1920 he joined the police, rising to the rank of *Major* in July 1935. He rejoined the Army in March 1936 and commanded various regiments. He was promoted to *Oberst* in October 1940. He took command of Mountain Regiment 139 in October 1941 and was appointed commander of the 6th Mountain Division in February 1942, when he was promoted to *Generalmajor*. Philipp remained commander of this division until August 1944, when he took command of the 8th Jäger Division new with the rank of *Generalleutnant*.

Knight's Cross: Awarded on 11 March 1945 as *Generalleutnant* and Commander of the 8th Jäger Division for his leadership while leading his division in Ukraine, the Carpathian Mountain area and Slovakia. From April he took over the leadership of the XXIX. Army Corps after its Commander, *General der Infanterie* Kurt Röpke, had been wounded. He surrendered to US troops on 10 May 1945 and ten days later he was handed over

Generalmajor Philipp with *Generalmajor* Georg Ritter von Hengl, who was awarded the Knight's Cross on 25 August 1941 as commander of Mountain Jäger Regiment 137.

to Soviet forces. He spent the next few years in Soviet prison camps near Krasnogork, Stalingrad and later in the dock in front of a Military Tribunal in the district of Stalino in Kiev. He was sentenced to twenty-five years in a labour camp on 30 October 1947 and was released on 7 January 1956, together with *Generaloberst* Rudolf Schmidt, *Generalleutnant* Hermann Boettcher and *Generalmajor* Karl-Richard Kossmann.

Rudolf Werner REICHERT

Generalleutnant

* 24 November 1893, Nebra, Querfurt
+ 10 March 1967, Bremen

Knight's Cross: Awarded on 11 March 1945 as *Generalmajor* and Commander of the 292nd Infantry Division for his leadership and bravery during the heavy fighting around Pinsk, Ostrów and Narev as part of the 2nd Army. During the last weeks of the war he withdrew his troops into Poland and his command was virtually destroyed in the Heiligenbeil Pocket in East Prussia in March 1945. Reichert was promoted to *Generalleutnant* only a few days before he surrendered to British troops on 8 May 1945 and he remained in Allied captivity until July 1947.

Rudolf Reichert joined the Army in November 1912 and saw action during the First World War with Infantry Regiment 152, winning both the Iron Cross 1st and 2nd Classes. He became an air war tactics instructor at the Naval Academy in Mürwik from June 1934 with the rank of *Hauptmann* and later served as course director. At the start of the Second World War he served as Commander of Infantry Regiment 67, now with the rank of *Oberstleutnant*, and from August 1942 he was Commander of Infantry Regiment 218. From March 1943 he took command of Field Headquarters 619 and was promoted to *Generalmajor* in November 1944 as commander of the 292nd Infantry Division on the Eastern Front.

Hans-Günther Georg von ROST

Generalleutnant

* 17 November 1894, Hannover, Germany
+ 23 March 1945 near Székesfehérvár, Hungary

Hans-Günther von Rost [right] saw action as a platoon leader and battery leader with Field Artillery Regiment 10 during the First World War. He remained in the Army after the war and from October 1935, with the rank of *Major*, he was appointed Commander of I. Horse Artillery Battalion and later served as adjutant with 4th Army Group Command in Leipzig and then Vienna. At the start of the Second World War he was serving as commander of Artillery Regiment 13, with the rank of *Oberst*, seeing action in Poland. From October 1940 his regiment was part of the 13th Panzer Division and from July 1942 he served on the staff of the Armed Forces Commander in the Netherlands. In March 1943, with the rank of *Generalmajor*, he served as Chief of the General Staff of Military District III in Berlin before taking command of the Reichsgrenadier Division Hoch-und Deutschmeister from June 1944.

Knight's Cross: Awarded on 21 March 1945 as *Generalleutnant* and Commander of *Reichs* Grenadier Division '*Hoch-und Deutschmeister*' for his excellent leadership, a good tactical brain and for actions in Hungary as part of Army Group South. He saw action on the Eastern Front between December 1944 and March 1945, fighting near Lake Balaton, Pécs and near Székesfehérvár in Hungary, where he was killed by Soviet tank fire.

Karl-Richard KOSSMANN

Generalmajor

* 28 March 1899, Uelzen
+ 12 June 1969, Goslar

Knight's Cross: Awarded on 23 March 1945 as *Oberst* and Commander of Panzer Grenadier Regiment 74 for action during a fighting retreat against Soviet forces through Silesia and Moravia. On 15 January the Soviets launched an attack with a strong tank force against the retreating German forces and conducted a half-hour artillery barrage against the 6th *Volksgrenadier* Division

Karl-Richard Kossmann entered the Army as a war volunteer with Fusilier Regiment 73 in 1917 and when the war was over he joined the *Freikorps*. He later returned to the Army, serving with Infantry Regiment 16, and was commissioned as a *Leutnant* in April 1922. Later he was attached to the Army General Staff and from November 1938 he served as an instructor at the War Academy in Berlin. From September 1939 he served on the Staff of the Quartermaster General of the Army and from January 1941 he served as Chief of Operations on the General Staff of the 15th Infantry Division with the rank of *Oberstleutnant*. From April 1942 until June 1944 he served as Chief of Staff to the Military Commander in France, and from November 1944 he served as commander of the 10th Panzer Grenadier Division with the rank of *Oberst*.

and other forces. In response the Germans sent out Kossmann's Panzer Grenadier Regiment together with Panzer Regiment 27 for a counter-attack and they were deployed in a trench network in local woods. The powerful counter-attack and barrage against the Soviets was too much and they suffered heavy losses; in thirty minutes the Germans destroyed fifty-one Soviet tanks and forced them to fall back. From February 1945 Kossmann was named as commander of the 10th Panzer Grenadier Division and saw action near Krakow in Poland, during the fighting retreat from the Vistula, at Goerlitz and in Silesia. He was promoted to *Generalmajor* on 20 April but things had changed and by now the Germans had lost many tanks themselves and two of his regiments had been virtually destroyed. Kossmann and his division were forced to retreat and remnants that included Kossmann himself surrendered to Soviet troops on 10 May 1945. He was held in Soviet captivity until 7 January 1956, when he returned to Germany.

Dipl. Ing. Johann Paul Friedrich DREKMANN

Generalleutnant

* 13 November 1893, Hamburg-Harburg
+ 09 March 1960, Mülheim, North Rhine-Westphalia

Knight's Cross: Awarded on 28 March 1945 as *Generalleutnant* and Commander of the 252nd Infantry Division, part of the XXIII. Army Corps, for his leadership during the heavy fighting near the Vistula River in north-eastern Poland between 31 January and 2 February 1945. A few days later Drekmann was involved in another offensive success near the village of Czaple, still in Poland, and he

Paul Drekmann entered the Army as a war volunteer in August 1914 with Fusilier Regiment 39 and was commissioned as a *Leutnant* a year later. From August 1915 he served as a company officer with Infantry Regiment 160 for the rest of the war. He stayed with the Army after the war, attending many courses and was promoted to *Rittmeister* in April 1928. From October 1935 he served as a battalion commander with Infantry Regiment 75, now with the rank of *Major*. He was attached to the Army Weapons Office and became Group Director for weapons testing, being promoted to *Oberst* in October 1940. From April 1942 he was commander of Infantry Regiment 34, then was promoted to *Generalmajor* in October 1943 and made commander of the 161st Infantry Division. Later he took command of Corps Detachment A on the Eastern Front, and in July 1944 was promoted to *Generalleutnant*.

achieved further success during the attack near Schwenten and the road north of this town was recaptured, which led to the Soviets retreating to reorganise themselves. He spent the last month of the war in the Reserves and in July 1945 he was taken prisoner by British forces, being released two years later.

Gerhard Fritz Franz FEYERABEND

Generalleutnant

* 29 April 1898, Dopsattel, Eastern Prussia
+ 6 November 1965, Rottach-Egern, Bavaria

Gerhard Feyerbend entered the Army with Field Regiment 82 in March 1916 and was taken ill three times in seven months. When the war was over he remained with the army. He served as battalion adjutant with Artillery Regiment 1 and was promoted to *Hauptmann* in April 1933. In May the following year he was appointed Chief of Operations on the Staff of the 1st Division. From October 1937 he served as Chief of Operations with the 24th Division and was promoted to *Oberstleutnant* in March 1939. The following year he served on the Staff of the General of Artillery and later as Chief of Operations on the Staff of the XXXX. Army Corps, seeing action on the in the Western campaign. He served with the 2nd Army from April 1941 and was promoted to *Oberst* at the end of the year. By August 1943 he was Chief of the General Staff of the 1st Army on the Western Front and he was promoted to *Generalmajor* in February 1944.

Knight's Cross: Awarded on 5 April 1945 as *Generalleutnant* and Commander of the 11th Infantry Division for his outstanding leadership during the Sixth Battle of Courland, Feyerabend saw further action against the Soviet 10th Guards Army. He was captured by Soviet troops on 10 May with the remains of his division and later found out while in a prison camp that his wife and daughter had both been killed by members of the Soviet military. He was finally released by his captors on 10 July 1947.

Harald Johann SCHULTZ

Generalmajor

* 10 November 1895, Westerotten, Riga, Latvia
+ 15 March 1957, Lübeck

Knight's Cross: Awarded on 5 April 1945 as *Generalmajor* and Commander of the 24th Infantry Division, part of the 16th Army, for his leadership during the Sixth Battle of Courland. He led his command across the Dobele–Frauenburg railway line in Latvia and was later forced to retreat to a hill position near the Viesata River. The success of the withdrawal was down to Schultz, who was also the commander of a battle group that had held the Josta Railway station for four days, which had given the Germans enough time to occupy and organise a new position. He was involved in some fierce fighting in the Courland area before surrendering to Soviet troops on 9 May 1945. He was sentenced to twenty-five years' imprisonment in a Soviet Gulag, being released early in October 1955 after a general amnesty.

Otto-Hermann Adolf BRÜCKER

Generalleutnant

* 17 October 1899, Berlin-Friedenau, Brandenburg
+ 12 December 1964, Weinheim, Baden-Württemberg

Knight's Cross: Awarded on 14 April 1945 as *Generalmajor* and Commander of the 6th Volks-Grenadier Division for his leadership during the intensive battles near Hessersdorf, Germany, from January 1945. Brücker was presented by *General der Panzertruppe* Friedrich Kirchner, Commanding General of the LVII. Panzer Corps, on 20 April 1945. On 20 February 1945 a battle group under his command was tasked with setting up a new front line and to

Otto-Hermann Brücker entered Army service with Pioneer Battalion 20 in March 1918, seeing little action during the war. He remained in the Army after the war, serving briefly in the *Freikorps*, and then attended various Army courses. He was commissioned as a *Leutnant* in May 1922. In October 1935, now with the rank of *Hauptmann*, he transferred to the General Staff of the 9th Division and in August 1938 he was promoted to *Major*. He was now serving as an intelligence officer with the II. Army Corps and from April 1940 he was Chief of Operations on the General Staff of the XXIV. Army Corps, being promoted to *Oberstleutnant* in November 1940. In April 1942 he was serving as Chief of Operations on the General Staff of the 7th Army, seeing action on the Eastern Front under the command of *Generalleutnant* Willibald Freiherr von Langermann und Erlencamp.

establish a new defensive position. However, during the reorganisation the enemy attacked and struck with an initial force of eight to ten tanks, with infantry penetrating the front near Hennersdorf from both sides. At the same time, more tanks entered the southern sector of Wünschendorf, a village about 10 miles away in Thuringia. Brücker's force was now up against thirty-five tanks, of which seven were destroyed or put out of action during the course of the day. He ordered his reserves to attack and they halted the Soviet advance, which bought time for the German forces to retreat towards Poland. Brücker managed to lead his troops towards Poland and Czechoslovakia, fighting now as part of *Generalfeldmarschall* Ferdinand Schörner's Army Group Centre. Brücker was promoted to *Generalleutnant* on 20 April and led his troops towards the Czech border. However, they could not escape the Soviets and had to surrender to them on 8 May 1945. Brücker and his men went into captivity, most of whom died, but Brücker survived and was released in October 1955.

Gustav Ludwig HUNDT

Generalleutnant

* 27 September 1894, Pfaffenhofen, Bavaria
+ 21 April 1945 near Opava, Slovakia

Knight's Cross: Awarded on 15 April 1945 as *Generalleutnant* and Commander of the 1st Ski *Jäger* Division for actions on the Eastern Front. Hundt had already distinguished himself in battle in early January 1945 during the capture of Torna

Gustav Hundt entered the Army in July 1913 with Field Artillery Regiment 31 and soon after attended War School in Metz. He was commissioned as a *Leutnant* in April 1914 and served as an adjutant and a battery officer, ending the war with the rank of *Oberleutnant*. He left the Army in 1920 and studied Political Science at University in Hamburg before returning to the Army in July 1934 with the rank of *Hauptmann*. He served with Artillery Regiment 30 and from September 1941 he was commander of his regiment and was promoted to *Oberst* in February 1942. Later that year he took command of the 30th Infantry Division, seeing action during the Russian campaign. In March 1944 he attended the 10th Divisional Leaders' Course and took command of the 340th Infantry Division from May. He was promoted to *Generalleutnant* in March 1945.

Vármegye and Szádudvarnok in Hungary as well as in the fighting around Szepsi. On 26 January he received orders to go to Rybnik, where he found just one battalion from his division available and launched a surprise attack at enemy forces that had been pinning down his division for some time. During the night the Russians suddenly attacked the city with strong forces, their only opposition being hastily assembled and straggler units. After making a deep penetration into the city, the enemy succeeded in reaching the city centre with support from several tanks. The situation had become threatening, with a very real danger that the enemy would assume total control over the city. Despite the frantic situation, Hundt was undeterred and visited every hotspot while escorted by a single officer to rally his troops. With great initiative and bravery, he fought at the head of his troops and personally led every counter-attack. His leadership was very successful and his troops recaptured all but a small part of the city. He then immediately organised the defence of Rybnik while his troops captured the remaining Soviet soldiers. Due to his accomplishments, the key crossroads of Rybnik were cleared of enemy troops, the Soviet objective of outflanking the 17th Army came to nothing and a continuous defensive line was created. However, on 21 April Hundt was reported as missing and his body was never found. After the war in June 1950 a German court declared him dead and his date of death was given as 21 April 1945.

Friedrich-Carl Walter RABE VON PAPPENHEIM

Generalleutnant

* 5 October 1894, Münster, North Rhine-Westphalia
\+ 9 June 1977, Hamm, North Rhine-Westphalia

Knight's Cross: Awarded on 30 April 1945 as *Generalleutnant* and Commander of the 97th *Jäger* Division for actions during the defensive fighting in Upper Silesia. On 8 March 1945 Rabe Von Pappenheim took part in the fighting near Raciborz in Poland and under his leadership his unit advanced far beyond its original attack objective. When Allied troops penetrated the front line near Szczyty in Poland on 28 March with sixty tanks, it was Rabe von Pappenheim who directed the blocking of the front near Krowiarki. During the evening of 31 March, following three days of fighting, the Soviets sent a strong tank force against the Germans. Although his men were exhausted, he managed to bring back their fighting spirit and they captured an important village from the enemy. He took over command of the 154th Infantry Division on 18 April but saw little action as his command had been virtually wiped out by Soviet forces. On 8 May, while in Pisek in Czechoslovakia, he was taken prisoner by US forces and in early June he was handed over to the Soviets. He was taken to the NKVD Prison Camp No. 27 at Krasnogorsk, and then to various other camps near Moscow before being tried by a court and being sentenced to twenty-five years' years hard labour on 3 July 1950. He was released, however, on 10 October 1955 after a general amnesty and returned to Germany.

Friedrich-Carl Rabe von Pappenheim entered the Army in August 1914 as a *Fahnenjunker* with Infantry Regiment 166. He was commissioned as a *Leutnant* in April 1915 and served as a machine-gun officer until the end of the war. He remained in the Army and served as a regimental adjutant. He later served with the 15th Mounted Regiment in Münster, where he was promoted to *Rittmeister* in April 1928. From 1935 he served in various Army departments and from October 1937 he served as Military Attaché at the German Mission in Brussels, now with the rank of *Major*. From June 1940 he served as commander of the 463rd and later the 436th Infantry Regiments, and from November 1941 he was Military Attaché of the German Mission in Budapest. Promoted to *Generalmajor* in August 1943, he was made leader of the 97th Jäger Division from December. He was confirmed as commander in February 1944 and was promoted to *Generalleutnant* five months later.

Ernst Friedrich BIEHLER

Generalmajor

* 7 June 1903, Ulm, Germany
+ 26 May 1997, Langensteinbach, Germany

Knight's Cross: Awarded on 9 May 1945 as *Generalmajor* and Fortress Commandant of Frankfurt an der Oder in recognition of his distinguished command during the heavy fighting in early 1945. Biehler had been serving as Chief of Operations of the Fortress Commandant of Frankfurt from 25 January 1945 and in April he took over from *Generalleutnant* Hermann Meyer-Rabingen as Fortress Commandant of Frankfurt. He was promoted to *Generalmajor* on 20 April and eight days later was wounded near Halbe in Berlin. He was not informed of his award of the Knight's Cross until after the war. The award recommendation from the field arrived without any justification at the Army Personnel Office on 20 April 1945. An approval of the award has never been found in the archives. According to the Award Association of the Knight's Cross, the decoration was awarded in accord with the Dönitz Directive, and is therefore not legal. Biehler was captured by Soviet troops on 28 April 1945 and taken into Soviet captivity. He was finally released under a general amnesty on 7 October 1955.

Ernst Biehler was attached to Infantry Regiment 13 from September 1923 and was commissioned as a *Leutnant* in April 1928. He was attached to Infantry Regiment *Ludwigsburg* from October 1934. Biehler was appointed company commander of Infantry Regiment 13 in October 1935, now with the rank of *Hauptmann*, and was assigned to the War Academy shortly after the German invasion of Poland in September 1939. He then attended various General Staff officer courses and from June 1940 he was intelligence officer with the 26th Infantry Division. From November he served in a similar capacity with the 24th Infantry Division in France and then from June 1941 he saw action in the Soviet Union. He was promoted to *Oberstleutnant* in April 1942 and from mid-1943 he took over command of Grenadier Regiment 31. In November 1943 he was appointed Chief of Operations of the 9th Luftwaffe Field Division and was promoted to *Oberst* in May 1944. He later became Chief of the General Staff of the XXVII. Army Corps before taking command of Grenadier Regiment 358 in September 1944.

Robert Josef MACHER
Generalmajor

* 18 November 1902, Munich
+ 22nd October 1949, Camp 159, Odessa, Ukraine

Knight's Cross: Awarded on 14 May 1945 as *Generalmajor* and Chief of the General Staff of Army High Command East Prussia (*Armeeoberkommando Ostpreußen*) in recognition of his distinguished command and service during the heavy fighting against Soviet forces. The Knight's Cross was awarded via a radio message from the Dönitz Government in Flensburg to the army headquarters of East Prussia. However, nothing has ever been found concerning this in any official records of the Army Personnel Office, so therefore the award is not valid since it was made after 8 May 1945, in accord with the Dönitz Directive, and is therefore not legal. Macher was arrested by Soviet forces in May 1945 and died while in prison in Ukraine.

Robert Macher was attached to the Royal Bavarian Cadet Corps from September 1915 and later served with a *Reichswehr* rifle regiment in Munich shortly after the war. He was commissioned as a *Leutnant* in December 1924 and was assigned to Army Headquarters in Regensburg until October 1935. He was appointed a General Staff Officer with the 10th Division at this time and was promoted to *Major* in June 1939. He was appointed Chief of Operations in the 73rd Infantry Division in August of that year. From March 1940 he served as Chief of Operations of the XXXXI. Infantry Corps and from June 1941 he was Liaison Officer with the 4th Romanian Army. He was promoted to *Oberstleutnant* in March 1942 while Chief of Operations with the 12th Army. In August he took over as Chief of the General Staff of the 2nd Army and was promoted to *Oberst* in January 1943.

Georg Heinrich RADZIEJ
Generalleutnant

* 7 January 1895, Pyskowice, Silesia
+ 13 May 1972, Frankfurt am Main, Germany

Knight's Cross: Awarded on 9 May 1945 as *Generalleutnant* and Commander of the 169th Infantry Division in recognition of his bravery and service on the

Georg Radziej entered the Army in October 1914 with Lower Silesian Infantry Regiment 154 and was commissioned as a *Leutnant* in September 1915. Later that year he served as Adjutant of the I. Battalion of his regiment and was wounded in October 1917, returning to duty in May 1918. He was the holder of both classes of the Iron Cross. He remained in the Army after the war, rising to the rank of *Oberleutnant* in July 1925. He was promoted to *Hauptmann* in February 1932 while serving on the Staff of group Command in Berlin. In October 1935 he was company commander with the 7th Infantry Regiment in Glatz and later served as an instructor at the War School in Dresden and later in Wiener-Neustadt. Promoted to *Oberstleutnant* in April 1939, he served as commander of the III. Battalion with Mountain Infantry Regiment 139 at the beginning of the Second World War. He later served as commander of Mountain Jäger Regiment 143 and from September 1943 he was commander of the 169th Infantry Division, now with the rank of *Generalmajor*.

Eastern Front. The award recommendation from the field arrived without any justification via teletype message at the Army Personnel Office on 20 April 1945. A written recommendation was promised but was never submitted. Radziej's name was never entered in the handwritten log of recommendations and an index card was not started. Therefore, from the point of view of the Award Association of the Knight's Cross, the award was approved as a result of the Dönitz Directive and is therefore illegal. Radziej was captured by Soviet forces near Kessel on 28 April 1945 and was later held in various prison camps, which included NKVD Camp No. 27 in Krasnogorsk, Camp No. 48 in Černcy, Ležnevo and later in Camp No. 185 in Butyrskaja-Gefängnis, Moscow. Radziej was tried by a Military Tribunal in Moscow on 28 June 1950 and sentenced to twenty-five years' hard labour, but he was released after a general amnesty on 7 October 1955.

Hans Rudolf Ludwig Otto VOIGT

Generalmajor

* 21 February 1896, Hannover, Germany
+ 26 April 1969, Frankfurt am Main, Germany

Knight's Cross: Awarded on 28 April 1945 as *Generalmajor* and Local Area Commander in Arnswalde, a town in West Pomerania, Poland, for distinguished service during the heavy fighting against the Soviets during the German retreat. There is no proof of this award in any of the surviving records in the German archives. The Award Association of the Knight's Cross recorded the following, 'Generalmajor Voigt is to be recognised as a recipient of the Knight's Cross, even if the formalities are not 100% in order.' Voigt at the time came under the command of the Commander-in-Chief of Army Group Vistula, *Reichsführer-SS* Heinrich Himmler, who could not authorise such an award. Therefore the date of the award was moved to much later and recorded as 28 April 1945 by *General der Infanetrie* Wilhelm Burgdorf, who was Chief of the Army Personnel Office but had no power to authorise such an award. Hence, the award was approved by the Award Association of the Knight's Cross after the war and therefore is illegal. Voigt surrendered to troops of the Western Allies on 4 May 1945 and remained in Allied captivity until his release in 1946.

Bibliography

Angolia, John R., *On the Field of Honor: A History of the Knight's Cross Bearers Volume 1*, San Jose, California, Roger James Bender, 1979.

Angolia, John R., *On the Field of Honor: A History of the Knight's Cross Bearers Volume 2*, San Jose, California, Roger James Bender, 1980.

Barnett, Correlli, edited by, *Hitler's Generals*, Weidenfeld & Nicholson, 1989.

Beevor, Antony, *Stalingrad*, Viking Press, 1998.

Binns, Stewart, *Barbarossa and the Bloodiest War in History*, Wildfire, 2021.

Bouysse, Grégory & Mark Spencer, *Encyclopaedia of the New Order. Knight's Cross of the Iron Cross Holders Part 1 September 1939–May 1940*, Author Publisher, 2021.

Bradley, Dermot, Karl-Friedrich Hildebrand & Markus Rövekamp, *Die Generale des Heeres 1921–1945 Band: 1–7*, Osnabrück, Bibili-Verlg, 1993–2004.

Brett-Smith, Richard, *Hitler's Generals*, Osprey, 1976.

Buttar, Prit, *Retribution. The Soviet Reconquest of Central Ukraine, 1943*, Osprey, 2019.

Buttar, Prit, *The Reckoning. The Defeat of Army Group South, 1944*, Osprey, 2020.

Caddick-Adams, Peter, *Monte Cassino. Ten Armies in Hell*, Arrow, 2013.

Chales De Beaulieu, W., *General Erich Hoepner. A Military Biography*, Casemate, 2021.

Carruthers, Bob Edited, *Hitler's Wartime Orders. The Complete Führer Directives 1939–1945*, Pen & Sword, 2018.

Clark, Alan, Barbarossa, *The Russian-German Conflict 1941–45*, Hutchinson, 1965.

Clark, Lloyd, *Blitzkrieg. Myth Reality and Hitler's Lightning War – France, 1940*, Atlantic Books, 2016.

Dimbleby, Jonathan, *Barbarossa. How Hitler Lost the War*, Viking, 2021.

Dixon, Jeremy, *The Knight's Cross with Oakleaves 1940–1945. Biographies and Images of the 889 Recipients Vols 1+2*, Schiffer Ltd, 2012.

Ellis, Frank, *The Stalingrad Cauldron. Inside the Encirclement and Destruction of the 6th Army*, University Press of Kansas, 2013.

Forczyk, Robert, *Where the Iron Crosses Grow. The Crimea 1941–44*, Osprey, 2014

Goralski, Robert, *World War II Almanac 1931–1945. A Political and Military Record*, London: Hamish Hamilton, 1981.

Hargreaves, Richard, *Blitzkrieg Unleashed. The German Invasion of Poland 1939*, Pen & Sword, 2008.

Hargreaves, Richard, *The Germans in Normandy*, Pen & Sword, 2006.

Hastings, Max, *Overlord. D-Day and the Battle for Normandy 1944*, Michael Joseph, 1984.

Hébert, Valerie G., *Hitler's Generals on Trial. The Last War Crimes Tribunal at Nuremberg*, University Press of Kansas, 2010.

Isaev, Alexey, *Hitler's Fortresses in the East. The Sieges if Ternopol, Kovel, Poznan & Breslau 1944–1945*, Pen & Sword, 2021.

Kursietis, Andris J., *The Fallen Generals: The Destruction of the German Officer Corps in World War II and its aftermath*, Netherlands, Andris J. Kursietis, 2015.

Lucas, James, *Hitler's Commanders. German Bravery in the Field 1939–1945*, Cassell & Co., 2000. Luther, Craig W.H. and David Stahel, *Soldiers of Barbarossa. Combat, Genocide, and Everyday Experiences on the Eastern Front, June–December 1941*, Stackpole Books, 2020.

MacLean, French L., *Quiet Flows the Rhine. German General Officer Casualties in World War II*, J.J. Fedorowicz Publishing, 1996.

Mallett, Derek R., *Hitler's Generals in America. Nazi POWs and Allied Military Intelligence*, University Press of Kentucky, 2013.

Manstein, Erich von, *Lost Victories*, Henry Regnery Company, 1958.

Marshall, Charles F., *The Rommel Murder. The Life and Death of the Desert Fox*, Stackpole Books, 1994.

May, Ernest R., *Strange Victory. Hitler's Conquest of France*, I.B. Tauris, 2000.

Mitcham, Samuel W., *The German Defeat in the East 1944–45*, Stackpole, 2007.

Mitcham, Samuel W., *Hitler's Field Marshals and their Battles*, Guild Publishing, 1988.

Mitcham, Samuel W., *The Men of Barbarossa. Commanders of the German Invasion of Russia, 1941*, Casemate Publishers, 2009.

Mitcham, Samuel W., *Panzer Commanders of the Western Front. German Tank Generals in WWII*, Stackpole, 2008.

Mitcham, Samuel W., *Panzers in Winter. Hitler's Army and the Battle of the Bulge*, Praeger Security International, 2006.

Mitcham, Samuel W., *Rommel's Lieutenants. The Men who Served the Desert Fox, France, 1940*, Stackpole, 2007.

Mitcham, Samuel W. & Gene Mueller, *Hitler's Commanders*, Leo Cooper, 1992.

Moorhouse, Roger, *Poland 1939. The Outbreak of World War II*, Basic Books, 2020.

Müller, Rolf-Dieter, *Enemy in the East. Hitler's Secret Plans to Invade the Soviet Union*, I.B. Tauris, 2015.

Nafziger, George F., The German Order of Battle. Infantry in World War II, London: Greenhill Books, 2000.

Nafziger, George F., *The German Order of Battle. Panzers and Artillery in World War II*, London: Greenhill Books, 1999.

Newton, Steven H., *Hitler's Commander. Field Marshal Walther Model – Hitler's Favourite General*, Da Capo Press, 2006.

Paget, R.T., *Manstein. His Campaigns and his Trial*, Collins, 1951.

Sadarananda, Dana v., *Beyond Stalingrad. Manstein and the Operations of Army Group Don*, Stackpole Books, 1990.

Scherzer, Veit, *Deustche Truppen im Zweiten Weltkrieg: Die Divisionen Band 2–7*, Scherzers Militaer Verlag, 2007–2011.

Scherzer, Veit, *Ritterkreuzträger 1939–1945*, Scherzers Militaer-Verlag Ranis, 2007.

Seaton, Albert, *The German Army 1933–1945*, Weidenfeld & Nicholson, 1982.

Shepherd, Ben H., *Hitler's Soldiers. The German Army in the Third Reich*, Yale University Press, 2016.

Stein, Marcel, *A Flawed Genius. Field Marshal Walter Model. A Critical Biography*, Helion & Company, 2010.

Stockert, Peter, *Die Eichenlaubträger 1940–1945 Band: 1–4*, Verlag Friedrichshaller Rundblick, 1997.

Taylor, Brian, *Barbarossa to Berlin: A Chronology of the Campaigns on the Eastern Front 1941 to 1945*, two volumes, Spellmount, 2003 & 2004.

Thomas, Franz & Günter Wegmann, *Die Ritterkreuzträger der Deutschen Wehrmacht 1939–1945 Band: 1–7*, Osnabrück, Biblio-Verlag 1987–2010.

Thomas, Franz & Günter Wegmann, *Die Ritterkreuzträger der Gebirgstruppe Band: 1–2*, Osnabrück, Biblio-Verlag 1993–94.